Brazil by British and Irish Authors

Brazil
by British and Irish Authors

Leslie Bethell

Centre for Brazilian Studies
University of Oxford

Leslie Bethell is Emeritus Professor of Latin American History, University of London, Director of the Centre for Brazilian Studies, University of Oxford and Fellow of St Antony's College, Oxford.

ISBN 0-9544070-1-6

© Leslie Bethell, 2003

Designed by Meg Palmer, Third Column
Printed by Lightning Source

Contents

	page
Preface	7
PART I • 1500–1808	11
16th and 17th centuries	13
18th and early 19th centuries	17
Part II • 1808–1945	29
Introduction	31
1808–1831	34
1831–1870	52
1870–1914	68
1914–1945	83
PART III • 1945–c. 2000	93
Introduction	95
1945–c. 1970	96
c. 1970–c. 2000	102
Indexes	127
Authors	129
Places	133

Preface

This guide to Brazil in books by British and Irish authors is divided into three parts along broadly chronological lines.

Part I offers a survey of the (relatively few) first hand descriptions of Brazil under Portuguese colonial rule by British and Irish visitors, most of whom did not stay very long and did not venture beyond the coastal towns, from the 16th century to the beginning of the 19th century. It concludes with the first comprehensive history of colonial Brazil, written by an Englishman who never visited Brazil: the poet Robert Southey.

Part II is a survey of the (many) books by British visitors to Brazil — and British residents in Brazil — from 1808, when the Portuguese Court, escorted by ships of the British Navy, transferred itself from Lisbon to Rio de Janeiro and opened Brazil to international trade (and foreign visitors), and especially from 1822 when Brazil declared its independence from Portugal, to the Second World War — a period of more than a century in which Britain was the pre-eminent political and economic power and also had considerable social, cultural and intellectual influence in Brazil.

Parts I and II together attempt to provide for the first time a comprehensive guide to the literature on Brazil by British and Irish writers from the 16th century to the early decades of the 20th century — a rich source for all who study Brazilian history. It makes full use of, but goes beyond, existing bibliographies which include the writings of British *viajantes*.*

---

*For example, Rubens Borba de Moraes and William Berrien, eds, *Manual bibliográfico de estudos brasileiros* (Rio de Janeiro: Gráfica Editora Souza, 1949), Rubens Borba de Moraes, *Bibliographia Brasiliana: a bibliographical essay on rare books about Brazil published from 1504 to 1900 and works of Brazilian authors of the colonial period* (1958; revised and enlarged edition, 2 vols, Los Angeles: Latin American Center, University of California; Rio de Janeiro: Livraria Kosmos Editora, 1983), Paulo Berger, *Bibliografia do Rio de Janeiro de viajantes e autores estrangeiros, 1531–1900* (Rio de Janeiro: Livraria São José, 1964), Bernard Naylor, *Accounts of nineteenth-century South America. An annotated checklist of works by British and United States observers* (London: Institute of Latin American Studies, 1969), Charles Griffin, ed., *Latin America. A guide to the historical literature* (Austin: University of Texas Press, for the Conference on Latin American History, 1971) and Edward J. Goodman, *The exploration of South America: An annotated bibliography* (New York: Garland Publishing, 1983).

It offers brief descriptions of the contents of each volume. And there are references to any MODERN EDITIONS and to any PORTUGUESE TRANSLATIONS.

Part III examines British writing on Brazil since 1945. While not neglecting accounts of Brazil by British travellers and independent authors in the second half of the 20th century, it focuses on the books (it was not possible to include journal articles, research papers and chapters in books) written by scholars in British universities in the post-war period, beginning with the work of Charles Boxer, Britain's greatest modern historian of colonial Brazil, and a few others during the 1950s and 1960s and continuing with the books of the 'Brazilianists' who began their academic careers in the aftermath of the Parry Report (1965) on Latin American Studies in British universities. The concern is primarily with the humanities and social sciences, excluding for the most part the life, environmental and medical sciences, except for multi-disciplinary studies of Amazonia, a field in which British scholars have made a particularly notable contribution.

Part III has inevitably less claim to comprehensiveness than do Parts I and II. There are so many books worthy of mention after c. 1970 that it was necessary to be somewhat selective. And for the most part descriptions are not provided for academic publications whose titles are normally self-explanatory. Most academic books published during the last twenty years or so are in any case still in print and/or relatively easy to locate.

Brazil by British and Irish authors is a much revised and much expanded version of an essay, 'A contribuição británico para estudo do Brasil', in Rubens Antonio Barbosa, Marshall C. Eakin and Paulo Roberto de Almeida, eds, *O Brasil dos Brasilianistas. Um guia dos estudos sobre o Brasil nos Estados Unidos, 1945–2000* (São Paulo: Editora Paz e Terra, 2002), published in English as *The British contribution to the study of Brazil* (University of Oxford Centre for Brazilian Studies, Working paper no. 37, 2003) and in Rubens Antonio Barbosa et al., eds, *Envisioning Brazil. A guide to Brazilian studies in the United States, 1945–2002* (Madison: University of Wisconsin Press, forthcoming, 2004). The author wishes to thank the many British colleagues who supplied information for the original essay from which this guide grew and especially John Hemming, John Dickenson, Peter Flynn and Oliver Marshall. Oliver Marshall, Research Associate of the Oxford Centre for

Brazilian Studies and author of *Brazil in British and Irish archives* published by the Centre in 2002, provided valuable research input in the preparation of this volume and took responsibility for the preparation of the volume for publication by the Centre. I am therefore particularly grateful to him.

Leslie Bethell
Centre for Brazilian Studies
Oxford
July 2003

PART I
1500–1808

16th and 17th centuries

Having 'discovered' Brazil in 1500 and begun the settlement of some coastal areas the Portuguese made every effort, not always successful, to keep out other Europeans, not least the British. Nevertheless, a number of British and Irish sailors, unlicensed traders, adventurers, privateers and pirates landed on the Brazilian coast during the 16th and early 17th centuries. They included, for example:

- **William Hawkins**, who was three times in Brazil during the years 1530–32;

- **Francis Drake**, who sailed along the Brazilian coast in 1578 at the start of his voyage round the world (1577–80);

- William Hawkins' nephew **William Hawkins** and the **Rev. Richard Madox**, who were members of Edward Fenton's abortive expedition to establish a spice trade in the Moluccas which called in Santa Catarina in 1582 and returning a year later landed in São Vicente for refitting;

- **Thomas Cavendish**, who in 1586 on the outward leg of the voyage that would make him only the second Englishman and third European (after Magalhaes and Drake) to sail round the world sacked Santos and São Vicente and who in December 1591 on a second expedition against the Spanish in the Pacific attacked São Vicente and other Portuguese settlements in Brazil, this time to be repulsed;

- **Anthony Knivet** who, after being shipwrecked following Cavendish's second attack on São Vicente and captured by the Portuguese, spent almost ten years in Brazil (1592–1601);

- **Sir Richard Hawkins**, grandson of the first William Hawkins, who visited Brazil, the third of this illustrious family of British sailors to do so, on his way to the South Seas in 1593;

- **Sir James Lancaster** who, like Cavendish, raided the coast of Brazil during the period of Spanish domination of Portugal, sacking Recife in 1595;

- **Bernard O'Brien**, an Irishman who lived on the lower Amazon in the 1620s.

Several journals and narratives by British and Irish adventurers which included first hand accounts of Brazil were published in **Richard Hakluyt**, *The principal navigations, voyages, traffics and discoveries of the English nation* (vol. I London, 1598; vol. II 1599; second edition, much expanded, in 3 volumes, with vol. III on the Americas, 1600; new expanded edition in 5 volumes, London, 1809) and **Samuel Purchas**, *Hakluytus posthumus or Purchas his pilgrimes. Containing a history of the world in sea voyages and land travels by Englishmen and others* (4 vols, 1625; 2nd ed., 20 vols, Glasgow, 1905–07), as well as in Theodore De Bry, *Grands voyages* (the first volume of the collection, both German and Latin versions, published in 1590, but continued by others for more than twenty years after De Bry's death in 1598). For example, Cavendish's account of his exploits on the coast of Brazil can be found in Hakluyt's *Principal navigations* vol. II, Lancaster's in Hakluyt vol. III, 'The admirable adventures and strange fortunes of Master Anthony Knivet, which went with Master Thomas Cavendish in his second voyage to the South Sea, 1591', in volume 4 of *Purchas his pilgrimes* (London, 1625).

The observations of Sir Richard Hawkins in his voyage to the South Seas in the year 1593, with its descriptions of various parts of Brazil, written in 1603–4, was first published in London in 1622 and then in *Purchas his pilgrimes* (1625). It was re-published by the recently founded Hakluyt Society in 1847 — the first volume published by the Society.

See also *The Hawkins' voyages during the reigns of Henry VIII, Queen Elizabeth and James I* edited with an introduction by Clements R. Markham (London: Hakluyt Society, 1878), *The voyages of Sir James Lancaster to Brazil and the East Indies, 1591–1613* edited with an introduction and notes by William Foster (London: Hakluyt Society, 1940), and *An Elizabethan in 1582. The diary of Richard Madox, Fellow of All Souls*, ed. Elizabeth Story Donno (London, 1976).

For 'Bernard O'Brien's account of Irish activities in the Amazon 1621–24' and other contemporary descriptions of English and Irish activities in the Amazon, see Joyce Lorimer, *English and Irish settlement on the River Amazon, 1550–1646* (London: Hakluyt Society, 1989).

There are two PORTUGUESE TRANSLATIONS of Anthony Knivet's *Adventures* (1625): *Revista do Instituto Histórico e Geográfico Brasileiro*, vol. XLI (1878), ed. Duarte Pereira (from the Dutch translation of 1706), and São Paulo, Editora Brasiliense (1947), ed. Guiomar de Carvalho Franco, with notes by Francisco de Assis Carvalho Franco (from the original English edition).

For Richard Hawkins' *Observations* (1622) in PORTUGUESE TRANSLATION, see E. San Martin, ed., *A viagem do pirata Richard Hawkins 1590–94. História autêntica da era dos descobrimentos* (Porto Alegre, 2001).

From the middle of the 17th century there is one Irish and one English account of a visit to Brazil:

- **Richard Fleckno(e)**, an Irish Catholic priest, poet, dramatist and adventurer, spent eight months in Rio de Janeiro, January–August 1649. *A relation of ten years travells in Europe, Asia, Affrique and America* (London, 1654; 2nd edition, 1657) includes an account of the voyage from Lisbon to Pernambuco and onwards to Rio de Janeiro in 1648, and sections headed 'of Brasil in general', 'of the town', 'of the country', 'of the savages' and 'of the commodities';

  PORTUGUESE TRANSLATION in Affonso de E. Taunay, *Visitantes do Brasil colonial* (São Paulo: Companhia Editora Nacional, 1933);

- **Edward Barlow**, *Journal of his life at sea ... from 1659 to 1703*, transcribed from the original manuscript by Basil Lubbock (2 vols, London, 1934) includes a short, but interesting, account of a five-months stay in Rio de Janeiro in 1663. Barlow's ship, the *Queen Catherine*, carried a cargo of wine from Madeira to Brazil only to find that the casks had all leaked during the eleven-week passage. In Rio, the *Queen Catherine* took on sugar, tobacco and other cargo for the return journey. The original journal, held by the National Maritime Museum in Greenwich, includes a fine watercolour depicting Rio and Guanabara Bay and another of Fernando de Noronha, an island that Barlow viewed from the sea.[1]

---

1 For a biography of Barlow, see A.G. Course, *A seventeenth-century mariner* (London, 1965).

And there is one account from the end of the 17th century:

- **William Dampier**, *A voyage to New-Holland, etc. in the year 1699* (2 parts, 1703, 1709; reprinted in his 'complete works', 4 vols, 1729). Dampier, pirate, adventurer, explorer and naturalist, spent a month in Salvador (Bahia). He describes the town's fortifications and garrison in some detail as well as churches, convents and houses, and the position of slaves. Also discussed is trade with Europe and Africa (overseen mainly by Portuguese merchants, but also by an Englishman) and the production of sugar, cotton, coconuts and other crops.

There are two MODERN EDITIONS of Dampier's *Voyage*: John Masefield, ed., 2 vols, London, 1906; J.A. Williamson, ed., London, 1939.

18th and early 19th centuries

In the 18th century an increasing number of British ships en route for the Pacific, India and later Australia and China, via the Cape of Good Hope or Cape Horn and the Magellan Straits, made Brazilian ports, and especially Rio de Janeiro and Santa Catarina, stopping places for wood, water and fresh food.

The circumnavigation of the world by the ships *Duke* and *Duchess* in 1708–11 produced two books of interest which include accounts of Brazil:

- **Woodes Rogers**, *A cruising voyage round the world* (London, 1712; 2nd ed. 1718);

- and **Edward Cooke**, *A voyage to the South Sea and round the world* (2 vols, London, 1712; 2nd ed.,1718).

The *Duke* and *Duchess* visited the coast of Rio de Janeiro in November 1708. Both authors left accounts of Ilha Grande and more detailed descriptions of Angra dos Reis and the gold trail heading inland.

There are MODERN EDITIONS of both Rogers' *Voyage* and Cooke's *Voyage*: London, 1928.

The last of the privateers to complete a circumnavigation was **George Shelvocke** whose *A voyage round the world by way of the Great South Sea, perform'd in the years 1719, 20, 21, 22* (London 1726; 2nd ed., edited by his son, 1757) includes a lengthy account of a visit to the island of Santa Catarina en route to China in 1719.

There is a MODERN EDITION of Shelvocke's *Voyage*: London, 1928.

John Atkins, *A voyage to Guinea, Brazil, & the West Indies in His Majesty's Ships the Swallow and Weymouth* (London, 1735) is a record of the travels in 1721–22 of John Atkins, a Royal Navy surgeon. Although Atkins visited both Pernambuco and Bahia, very little is said of these ports. For Brazil, however, the value of this book essentially relates to the considerable detail given to the African slave trade and to the account of the ocean voyage from West Africa to Brazil.

Several accounts of **George Anson**'s circumnavigation of the world (1740–44) during the war with Spain, perhaps the most important voyage of exploration between those of Sir Francis Drake and Captain Cook, include descriptions of the island of Santa Catarina which Anson's fleet of five ships touched in December 1740 on its outward journey to the Pacific 'to distress the Spaniards in those parts':

- *A Voyage round the world in the years 1740, 41, 42, 43, 44 by George Anson Esq., commander in chief of His Majesty's ships sent upon an expedition to the South Seas* (London, 1748), a volume compiled from Anson's papers by **Richard Walter**, the chaplain of the HMS *Centurion*, is the fullest account, including a detailed description of the 'advantages' and 'inconveniences' of Santa Catarina and much information on Brazil in general.

  There are numerous MODERN EDITIONS in several languages as well as English.[2]

- *Log of the* Centurion *based on the original papers of Captain Philip Saumarez on board the H.M.S.* Centurion, *Lord Anson's flagship* (edited by Leo Heaps, London, 1973) includes lengthy accounts of the days spend in Santa Catarina. **Philip Saumarez**, from the island of Guernsey, was Anson's young first lieutenant.

- **John Bulkeley** and **John Cummins**, *A voyage to the South Seas, in the years 1740–41* (London, 1743) includes a brief entry on Santa Catarina. Buckeley and Cummins' ship, the *Wager*, was shipwrecked during passage through the Straits of Magellan the following year and they returned home via Brazil, providing a description of Rio de Janeiro in April–May 1742.

  MODERN EDITION: edited, with introduction and notes, by Arthur D. Howden Smith, London, 1927.

  PORTUGUESE TRANSLATION: Rio de Janeiro, Companhia Brasil Editora, 1936.

---

2 See also Glyn Williams, *The prize of all the oceans. The dramatic story of Commander Anson's voyage round the world* (New York, 1999), and especially the appendices on sources.

- **John Young**, *An affecting narrative of the unfortunate voyage and catastrophe of H.M.S. Wager* (London, 1751). Young returned home with Buckeley and Cummins and also provides a description of Rio de Janeiro in 1742.

Mrs Nathaniel Kindersley, a widow of a British army officer, was the first woman known to have written an account of a visit to Brazil: *Letters from the island of Teneriffe, Brazil, the Cape of Good Hope, and the East Indies* (London, 1777). She called at Salvador (Bahia) on her way to India in 1764, staying on-shore with a French surgeon and his Portuguese wife. The book includes a lengthy description of Salvador, a place that failed to impress Mrs Kindersley.

John Byron, *A voyage round the world, in His Majesty's Ship The Dolphin, commanded by the Honourable Commandore Byron* (London, 1767) includes descriptions of Rio de Janeiro recorded during a six week period in September–October 1764 while the ship was in port 'wooding, watering and caulking'. A meeting between Commodore Byron (grandfather of the poet) and the viceroy is described, as are the local fortifications, the slave market, churches and convents and food supplies. Byron had served with Anson twenty years earlier and had been shipwrecked on the *Alert*.

MODERN EDITION: Robert E. Gallagher, ed., *Byron's journal of his circumnavigation 1764–66*, Cambridge, for the Hakluyt Society, 1964.
PORTUGUESE TRANSLATION: Bahia, Typographia do Correio Mercantil, 1836.

James Forbes visited Rio de Janeiro in June–October 1765 on his way to join the East India Company in Bombay, where he lived for 17 years. Volume one of Forbes' *Oriental memoirs* (4 vols, London, 1813) includes a brief general description of the city, its vegetation, inhabitants and water supply.

At the beginning of the first of its famous voyages of circumnavigation (1768–71), HMS *Endeavour* under **Captain James Cook** spent several weeks in Brazil, November–December 1768. Cook was accompanied by the young botanist (and future president of the Royal Society, 1778–1820) **Joseph Banks**. Banks brought with him his assistant, the Swedish botanist Daniel Solander, a pupil of Carl Linnaeus, and two official artists: the 22 year old **Sydney Parkinson** and Alexander Buchan, who both died before the voyage was completed. Volume two of *An account of the voyages undertaken by order of his present Majesty for making discoveries in the Southern Hemisphere* (3 vols, London, 1773; 3rd edition, 4 vols, 1785) edited at the request of the admiralty by **John Hawkesworth**, includes an account of Cook's voyage round the world based on his own *Journal* as well as the papers of Banks and others. It records details of the *Endeavour*'s time in Rio de Janeiro, with general observations concerning the inhabitants, church and the administration of the city, the harbour, availability of food, gold and precious stones and currency and comments on the frequent murders and the lax morals of women. See also James Cook, *The three voyages of Captain James Cook round the world, complete in seven volumes*, Vol. I (London, 1821).

- *The Endeavour journal of Sir Joseph Banks*, vol. 1, ed. J.C. Beaglehole (Sydney, 1962), and *The journals of Captain Cook on his voyages of discovery*. ed. J.C. Beaglehole (London: Hakluyt Society, 1974) are the best of many MODERN EDITIONS.

    PORTUGUESE TRANSLATIONS of Captain Cook's *Journal*: Lisbon, Typografia Rollandiana, 1819, and *Revista Maritima Brasileira*, nos 7–12, 1953, ed. Albertino Pinheiro.

- **Sydney Parkinson** left *A journal of a voyage to the South Seas* (London, 1773), which features an extremely brief account of his time in Rio de Janeiro, and (much more important) the first significant body of scientific drawings of the flora and fauna of Brazil (more than 900, mostly held in the Natural History Museum, London).[3]

Several descriptions of Rio de Janeiro resulted from the visit in August–September 1787 of the 'First Fleet' (eleven ships with over two hundred officers and men transporting over seven hundred convicts, a quarter of them women, to New South Wales) under the command of Sir Arthur Phillip, first governor of New South Wales who had previously served in the Portuguese Navy for four years, which initiated the colonisation of Australia:

---

[3] See D.J. Carr, ed., *Sydney Parkinson. Artist of Cook's Endeavour Voyage* (London, 1983).

- **Arthur Phillip**, *The voyage of Governor Phillip to Botany Bay* (London, 1789) has an entire chapter on Rio de Janeiro.

  MODERN EDITION: edited, with introduction and notes, by James J. Auchmuty, Sydney, Royal Australian Historical Society, 1970.

- **Watkin Tench**, *Narrative of an expedition to Botany Bay* (London, 1789).

  MODERN EDITION: edited, with introduction and notes, by L.F. Fitzhardinge, Sydney, 1961.

- **John White**, *Journal of a voyage to New South Wales* (London, 1790). White was the fleet's chief surgeon and provides one of the most detailed descriptions of Rio de Janeiro at the end of the 18th century.

- **John Hunter**, *An historical journal of the transaction at Port Jackson and Norfolk Islands* (London, 1793). Hunter was captain of HMS *Syrius* and a future governor of New South Wales.

  MODERN EDITION: edited, with introduction and notes, by John Bach, Sydney, Royal Australian Historical Society, 1968.

- *A voyage to New South Wales. The journal of Lieut. William Bradley of H.M.S. Syrius, 1786–1792* (Sydney, 1969). The *Journal*, which was first published as a facsimile edition by the Public Library of New South Wales, includes, as well as a short account of visiting the city, five of **William Bradley**'s watercolours of views of Rio de Janeiro.

  PORTUGUESE TRANSLATION: *Diário e aquarelas: Rio de Janeiro, agosto de 1787* (Rio de Janeiro: Arte e História, 2000).[4]

Rio de Janeiro became a regular port of call of Australia-bound convict ships.[5] A visit to Rio de Janeiro in 1791 by the *Albemarle* to take on

---

4 See also Victor Crittenden, *The voyage of the First Fleet 1787–1788, taken from contemporary accounts* (Canberra, 1981) and Bernard Smith and Alwyne Wheeler, *The art of the First Fleet* (New Haven, 1988).

5 An entertaining account of the transportation to Australia in 1789 of 237 English female convicts, mainly prostitutes and petty thieves, is found in Siân Rees *The Floating Brothel* (London, 2001). The book includes a chapter recounting the experiences of the convicts in Rio de Janeiro, where some of the more privileged women were permitted to disembark.

supplies of water, fruit, beef and other food for over 300 convicts is described by **George Barrington**, a convicted thief ('the prince of pickpockets') from Ireland sentenced to serve seven years in Botany Bay, in *An account of a voyage to New South Wales* (3rd edition, London, 1795).

Lord Macartney's three-week visit to Brazil in November–December 1792 on his way to China as Britain's first ambassador also produced some noteworthy accounts of Rio de Janeiro:

- **Sir George Staunton**, *Authentic account of an embassy from the King of Great Britain to the Emperor of China* (2 vols, London, 1797). Staunton was Macartney's secretary. His book provides, along with that of John White, one of the best descriptions of Rio de Janeiro at the end of the 18th century.

- **John Barrow**, *Voyage to Cochinchina in the years 1792 and 1793* (London, 1806; 2nd revised edition, 2 vols, Paris, 1807, with notes, maps and illustrations). The fourth chapter of Barrow's narrative is devoted to Rio de Janeiro with a description of the port and landing facilities, an explanation of how the city was supplied with water, a discussion as to whether it was more cost effective to import slaves or breed them locally and an account of local manners and morals, especially in relation to women. The book's fifth chapter is a general overview of Brazilian history and geography. In the French edition the translator Conrad Malte-Brun, author of *Annales des voyages, de la geographie et de l'histoire* (Paris, 1809–14), replaced Barrow's chapter five with a chapter of his own.

- **Aeneas Anderson**, *A narrative of the British embassy to China in the years 1792, 1793 and 1794* (Dublin, 1795).

There are two interesting accounts of Brazil in books published at the end of the 18th century:

- **James Wilson**, *A missionary voyage to the Southern Pacific Ocean performed in the years 1796, 1797, 1798 in the ship Duff commanded by Captain James Wilson, compiled from* *journals of the officers and missionaries* (London, 1799), republished in *The life and dreadful sufferings of Captain James Wilson in various ports of the globe* (Portsea, 1810). See also **John Griffin**, *Memoirs of Captain James Wilson* (3rd ed., London, 1819).

The *Duff*, which was transporting thirty members of the London Missionary Society to Tahiti, anchored in Guanabara Bay for eight days in November 1796.

- **James George Semple Lisle**, *The Life of Major J.G. Semple Lisle; containing a faithful narrative of his alternate vicissitudes of splendor and misfortune* (London, 1799).

  Lisle, a convicted fraudster, was sentenced to deportation to Australia. During the voyage, despite Lisle's warnings to the ship's captain, a mutiny broke out. Lisle was allowed off the ship in a small boat and landed in Rio Grande do Sul. Lisle travelled northwards through Brazil to Bahia in 1797, eventually making his way to Tangiers where he surrendered to the British authorities. In his memoirs, impressions of Bahia and Rio de Janeiro are well covered, but especially interesting are general descriptions of Laguna in Santa Catarina and of the Portuguese, Indian and black populations of rural Rio Grande do Sul and the province's small settlements of Torres, Porto Alegre and Mostardes.

Finally, there are several accounts by British and Irish visitors to Brazil in the early years of the 19th century:

- **John Turnbull**, *A voyage round the world in the years 1800, 1801, 1802, 1803, and 1804* (London, 1805, 3 vols; 2nd ed., 1813).

  In 1800 Turnbull's ship called at Salvador with a leaking hull but the authorities believed the true mission was espionage. Turnbull, a merchant sailor, devotes a chapter to Salvador and describes a meeting with the viceroy as well as the physical appearance of the town, especially its dockyard and churches.

- **Thomas Lindley**, *Narrative of a voyage to Brasil* (London, 1805).

  Lindley, a British merchant, left Cape Town for Rio de

Janeiro in 1801 with surplus stock. Due to storm damage, his ship called at Salvador in 1802, whereupon he was promptly arrested on charges of smuggling under laws that prevented foreigners from trading in Brazil. Lindley was held for some ten months — rather casually imprisoned, since he was given opportunities to explore Salvador as well as to travel south to Porto Seguro. The journal records Lindley's experiences both in and out of prison, and describes aspects of life in Bahia, including the local Portuguese and British communities, religion, food and clothing.

PORTUGUESE TRANSLATION: São Paulo, Companhia Editora Nacional, Coleção Brasiliana, 1969.

- **James Tuckey**, *An account of a voyage to establish a colony at Port Phillip in the Bass Strait, on the south coast of New South Wales, in His Majesty's Ship Calcutta in the years 1802–3–4* (London, 1805).

  Tuckey, an Irish junior naval officer, spent twenty days in Brazil in May–June 1803 en route to Australia and wrote interestingly on social life, trade, politics, the police and courts. Approximately half the book is devoted to Rio de Janeiro with excellent descriptions of the landscape and urban environment. Tuckey was impressed by the city's water supply and described in some detail churches, the viceroy's palace and houses of the wealthy (their decoration was said to 'disgust the eye'). Especially interesting are Tuckey's detailed observations regarding women in the city — girls' schooling, the common practice of abortion and (until no more than twenty years of age) their beauty.

- **Sir George Mouat Keith**, *A voyage to South America and the Cape of Good Hope* (London, 1810; revised and expanded, 1819).

  Keith, a Royal Navy commander, describes the Brazilian port calls of HMS *Protector* in 1805. 'Never was a place of equal extent and importance so dirty, miserable and disgusting', he wrote of Salvador during the month that he spent there. But he found Rio de Janeiro more agreeable, describing positively that city's layout, its water supply, population and nearby farms. Confusing later historians, much of what he wrote was, however, transcribed from the earlier accounts of Louis Antoine Bougainville (1767) and James Cook (1768).

- **James Hardy Vaux**, *Memoirs of James Hardy Vaux* (2 vols, London, 1819).

   Vaux includes recollections of Rio de Janeiro, where he stopped for three months in May–August 1807 on his return to England from Australia. (He had been transported there some years earlier for embezzlement, and was to be transported again — twice!) Vaux recalls his days of leisure in Rio, and describes in particular religious processions and the slave market.

   MODERN EDITION: edited, with introduction and notes, by Noel MacLachlan, London, 1964.

- **Thomas O'Neill**, *A concise and accurate account of the proceedings of the squadron under the command of Rear Admiral Sir Will. Sidney Smith, K.C., in effecting the escape, and escorting the Royal Family of Portugal to the Brazils* (London, 1809).

   Under threat of invasion by Napoleon the Portuguese royal family and the Portuguese government evacuated Lisbon in November 1807 — in 24 warships and several merchant vessels — and were escorted across the Atlantic first to Salvador and then Rio de Janeiro by six British warships under the command of Admiral Sir Sidney Smith. O'Neill, a lieutenant on board HMS London, offers a lively first hand account of the chaotic and desperate scenes of the departure, the Atlantic voyage and arrival in Brazil.

Extracts from many British and Irish accounts of Rio de Janeiro during the period of Portuguese colonial rule can be found in PORTUGUESE TRANSLATION in two volumes edited by Jean Marcel Carvalho Franca: *Visões do Rio de Janeiro colonial. Antologia de textos, 1531–1800* (Rio de Janeiro, 1999) — accounts by Flecknoe, Barlow, Young, Byron,

Forbes, Cook, Phillip, White, Tench, Barrington, Staunton, Barrow, Anderson, Wilson and Lisle — and *Outras visões do Rio de Janeiro colonial. Antologia de textos, 1582–1808* (Rio de Janeiro, 2000) — accounts by Knivet, Bulkeley and Cummins, Parkinson, Hunter, Bradley, Tuckey, Keith, Vaux and O'Neill.

SOUTHEY'S HISTORY OF BRAZIL

The first history of Brazil under Portuguese colonial rule to treat the entire three centuries from the beginning of the 16th century to the early 19th century, and based on extensive research, was written by the young English revolutionary poet (and future poet laureate) **Robert Southey**, who had also never visited Brazil. The first volume of what became a three-volume *History* was published in 1810, two years after the Portuguese court had moved to Brazil, but he had begun work on the project more than a decade earlier.

In 1796 Southey (age 22) had spent three and a half months visiting his uncle the Rev. Herbert Hill, Anglican chaplain to the British factory (the community of British merchants), first in Oporto, then in Lisbon. He returned for 15 months in 1800–01. Hill was a great collector of Portuguese rare books and manuscripts. And it was in his uncle's library — and from 1803 back in England at his house in Keswick, in the Lake District, which he shared with Samuel Taylor Coleridge — that Southey began to write '[a] great historical work, the History of Portugal'. 'On Portugal I am probably better informed than any other foreigner, and as well informed as any Portuguese', he claimed in 1806. He planned an 11- or 12-volume history of Portugal itself and of the Portuguese in Asia and Brazil, the Jesuits in Japan, the literary history of Spain and Portugal and the history of the monastic orders. Work on the history of the Portuguese in the New World was brought forward following the British capture of Buenos Aires in 1806. 'The times being South America mad,' he wrote in December 1806, 'any account of Brazil instead of being the last work in the series must be the first.' The flight of the Portuguese court to Rio de Janeiro in 1807–08 to avoid falling into the hands of Napoleon reinforced this decision. His *History of Brazil* became the first part — and, although he continued to work on it until his death in 1843, the only part — of a projected *History of Portugal* to be published.

The three quarto volumes of Southey's *History of Brazil* (London, 1810, 1817, 1819) ran to more than 2,300 pages (with a concluding 'View of the State of Brazil' alone close to 200 pages). The first volume dealt with the territorial occupation of Brazil by the Portuguese (to 1640), the second with the Dutch occupation of northeast Brazil in the second quarter of the 17th century and their expulsion in 1654 and Portuguese relations with the Brazilian Indians, the third with territorial expansion north, south and west in the 18th century, the expulsion of the Jesuits, social institutions and the roots of what Southey saw as a future autonomous nation state. A revised edition of the first volume published in 1822 added a hundred pages more.

'What I have done,' Southey wrote in 1818, 'is in many parts imperfect; it is nevertheless even now a great achievement ... and centuries hence, when Brazil shall have become a great and prosperous country which one day it must be, I shall be regarded there as the first person who ever attempted to give a consistent form to its crude, unconnected and neglected history.' And in 1819, 'It will ... communicate to the Brazilians, when they have become a powerful nation, much of their history which would otherwise have perished. It will be to them what the works of Herodatus is to Europe.' Byron, however, famously described it as 'the best remedy for insomnia' he knew. And even Southey began to have his doubts: about the forthcoming third volume, he thought at most twenty people in England and half a dozen in Portugal and Brazil would read it avidly and with pleasure; perhaps fifty would buy it. Southey gained a reputation as an authority on Portugal and Brazil subjects. He was asked for advice by several British authors writing books on Brazil at this time, for example Henry Koster (see p. 37), John Luccock (see p. 36) and James Henderson (see p. 42).*

Southey's great *History*, much admired by later historians of colonial Brazil such as Capistrano de Abreu and Oliveira Lima, was published almost half a century before Varnahagen's classic *História geral do Brasil antes da sua separação e independência de Portugal* (2 vols, 1854–57), based on documents in the Torre do Tombo archive in Lisbon. Southey's *History* was somewhat eclipsed by Varnhagen's (though Capistrano de Abreu judged it superior 'in form, in conception, in perception').

Southey's *History* was first published in PORTUGUESE, reduced and in an inaccurate translation by Luiz Joaquim de Oliveira e Castro, in six volumes: Paris and Rio de Janeiro, B L Garnier, 1862. There have been several later editions, all based on the Oliveira e Castro translation, most recently in three volumes: Belo Horizonte and São Paulo, Editora Itatiaia/Editora da Universidade de São Paulo (Edusp), Coleção Reconquista do Brasil, nova série, vols, 67–69, 1981.

There is no modern critical edition of Southey's *History of Brazil* in either English or Portuguese.

---

* Joaquim de Souza Leão, 'Southey and Brazil', *The Modern Language Review*, vol. 38, no. 3, 1943, pp. 181–91. See also Joaquim de Souza Leão, ed., 'Cartas de Robert Southey a Theodore Koster e a Henry Koster (anos de 1804 a 1819)', *Revista do Instituto Histórico e Geográfico Brasileiro* vol. 176 (1943); R.A. Humphreys, *Robert Southey and his History of Brazil* (23rd Annual Canning House Lecture, London, 1978); and especially Maria Odila Leite de Silva Dias, *O fardo do homem branco: Robert Southey, historiador do Brasil* (São Paulo, 1974), a brilliant analysis of Southey's essentially conservative ideology and the political, intellectual and cultural context in which the *History* was written.

PART II
1808–1945

Introduction

For more than a century — from the dramatic events of 1807 in the Iberian Peninsula during the Napoleonic Wars, which led to the transfer of the Portuguese court from Lisbon to Rio de Janeiro and the opening of Portugal's American colony to international trade and investment and eventually in 1822 to Brazilian independence, to the First World War and, to a lesser extent, to the 1929 World Depression — Britain was the dominant external actor in the economic and political affairs of Brazil and a not insignificant influence on Brazilian society and culture.

Britain was the principal source of a whole range of manufactured consumer goods (particularly textiles), intermediate and capital goods and some key raw materials (especially coal). Britain was the principal source of capital — loans (Rothschilds were throughout the Brazilian government's principal agents) and direct investment in Brazilian infrastructure (mainly railways and public utilities). British ships carried the produce (mainly coffee) exported from Brazil, albeit less to the British market than to the United States and other markets throughout the world. For Brazil the 'long' 19th century was *o século inglês*.

It is not difficult to explain why Britain was so dominant in Brazil during the 19th century — and after. In the first place, Britain had been 'present at the creation'. The foundations of Britain's political, commercial and financial pre-eminence were firmly laid at the time of the formation of the independent Brazilian state. Secondly, from 1815 until 1870 Britain exercised an unchallenged global hegemony and at least until 1914 a somewhat less secure global supremacy. The British Navy ruled the waves. Thirdly, and most importantly, Britain, the 'first industrial nation', was the 'workshop of the world', more than half the world's merchant shipping was British and the City of London was the world's major source of capital.

As early as the 1820s there were sizeable British communities in Rio de Janeiro and the other major coastal towns of Brazil. At the head of these communities were Britain's diplomats and the representatives — some transient, some becoming permanent residents — of more than a hundred London and Liverpool merchant houses. They were joined in the second half of the 19th century by the managers and engineers of

British-owned railways, port facilities, urban transport systems and water, sewage and drainage, gas and eventually electricity companies, the office staff of banks and shipping and insurance companies, and skilled workers in workshops, mines and factories.

On the eve of the First World War Britain remained economically pre-eminent in Brazil: it was the principal holder of the Brazilian public debt, the principal investor in Brazil, and Brazil's principal trading partner. During the first half of the 20th century, however, Britain's share of the Brazilian market and Britain's share of direct foreign investment in Brazil gradually declined. This was in large part, of course, a consequence of Britain's overall relative economic decline. Britain's share of world manufacturing output and world trade fell. New York replaced London as the world's main capital market. And the damaging effects of two world wars on the British economy cannot be overestimated: Britain's export trade as a whole collapsed due to shipping shortages and the exigencies of wartime production; and not only was there no new investment overseas, British capital began to be withdrawn from many parts of the world. At the same time, in the aftermath of the 1929 Depression Britain increasingly strengthened its commercial and financial ties with the Empire, and especially with the Dominions, at the expense of Latin America.

The weakening of Britain's position in Brazil was also a consequence of economic and, to a lesser extent, social and political change in Brazil itself. Brazil began to develop its own manufacturing industries during the half century from 1880, a process which accelerated during the depression years of the 1930s. Brazil could itself produce many of the goods that had dominated Britain's export trade for more than a century and now required technologically more sophisticated manufactured and capital goods. Britain was a prisoner of its 19th-century past and had great difficulty adapting long-established patterns of trade and investment to the changing needs of Brazil.

Finally, Britain faced a powerful competitor for pre-eminence in Brazil. As the United States overtook Britain as the world's leading industrial and creditor nation it steadily increased its trade with, and investment in, its Latin American neighbours — first Mexico, Central America and the Caribbean, then the Andean republics and finally the Southern Cone and Brazil. By 1930 the US had replaced Britain as Brazil's main trading partner. By 1945 the US had also replaced Britain as Brazil's main source of capital. Moreover, during the Second World War political and cultural ties between the United States and Brazil had been enormously strengthened. If for Brazil the 19th century (and even the early 20th century) was predominantly British, the 20th century had become predominantly American.

This close relationship between Britain and Brazil from 1808 to the First World War, which was to some extent maintained during the inter-war years, produced a large number of books by British residents in Brazil and British visitors to Brazil:

- *mineralogists* (e.g. John Mawe);

- *merchants* (e.g. John Luccock and John Armitage);

- *sugar planters* (e.g. Henry Koster);

- *naval officers* (e.g. Admiral Sir Sidney Smith, Lord Cochrane, Robert Fitzroy, William Webster, Edward Wilberforce) — and their wives (Maria Graham);

- *diplomats* (e.g. Sir William Gore Ouseley, William Christie, Sir Richard Burton, James Bryce, Ernest Hambloch) — and their relatives (Henry Chamberlain), secretaries (Alexander Caldcleugh) and chaplains (Robert Walsh);

- *naturalists* (e.g. William Swainson, Charles Waterton, Charles Darwin, George Gardner, Alfred Russel Wallace, Henry Walter Bates, Richard Spruce, Henry Wickham);

- *missionaries* (e.g. John Candler and Wilson Burgess, Kenneth Grubb, Thomas Duncan, Horace Banner);

- *newspaper owners and editors* (e.g. William Scully, the Mulhalls) and journalists (e.g. Charles Domville-Fife, W.H. Koebel);

- *employees of navigation and railway companies* (e.g. William Hadfield, Charles Barrington Brown and William Lidstone, Thomas Plantagenet Bigg-Wither, Joseph Froude Woodoffe);

- *civil engineers* (e.g. Edward Mathews, James Wells, Hastings Charles Dent, J.P. Wileman);

- *explorers* (e.g. Robert and Richard Schomburgk, Percy Harrison Fawcett, Peter Fleming);

- *travel writers* (e.g. H.M. Tomlinson, Rudyard Kipling, Evelyn Waugh).

Based on a wealth of first hand knowledge and experience of Brazil these books are a fundamental source for the history of Brazil in the 19th and early 20th centuries.

1808–1831

Sir William Sidney Smith, *Memoirs*, edited by Edward Howard (2 vols, London, 1839).

Admiral Sir Sidney Smith, who had left the convoy transferring the Portuguese court to Brazil at Madeira, arrived in Rio de Janeiro in May 1808 to re-take command of the British fleet now stationed there. He remained in Rio until July 1809. Volume two of his *Memoirs* includes copies of letters relating to the transfer of the court and political intrigues in Rio, especially in relation to regulations governing British commercial interests, as well as a transcription of Thomas O'Neill's account (see above).

John Barrow, *The life and correspondence of Admiral Sir William Sidney Smith* (2 vols, London, 1848).

Volume two includes letters relating to the evacuation of Lisbon, the state of political parties in Brazil, Portuguese relations with the Rio de la Plata and the British–Portuguese attack on French forces at Cayenne launched from Pará.

John Parish Robertson and **William Parish Robertson**, *Letters from Paraguay* (2 vols, London, 1838).

The Robertsons were Scottish brothers with long-time business merchant interests in South America. Volume one includes letters written in 1808 by one of the brothers in Rio de Janeiro where he arrived in October on the HMS *Ajax*. The city's customs' house and docks are described in detail. The apparent absence of women — kept in 'Moorish seclusion' — interests the author. Also of interest are observations concerning slaves at the Campo Santa Ana, with a discussion of their various national or tribal origins.

Andrew Grant, *History of Brazil, comprising a geographical account of that country, together with a narrative of the most remarkable events which have occurred there since its discovery* (London, 1809; revised and expanded edition in French, St Petersburg, 1811).

This book is as much a guide for travellers and merchants as a history, with chapters on winds and currents for crossing the Atlantic and the Brazilian provinces' physical geography, manufactures and agriculture and fortifications. But six chapters examine Brazil's colonial history (Amerindian society, 'discovery and settlement', Portuguese, French and Dutch colonial activities, the slave trade and civil and ecclesiastical governance). Grant, who had never visited Brazil, was a doctor. There is an appendix detailing medical hints for Europeans emigrating to Brazil, with severe warnings about the climate.

John Mawe, *Travels in the interior of Brazil, particularly in the gold and diamond districts of that country* (London, 1812 and Philadelphia, 1816; 2nd revised and expanded edition, London, 1821).

Mawe, a mineralogist from Derbyshire, left England in August 1804 for the Rio de la Plata, arrived in Brazil (Santa Catarina) in September 1807 and then travelled overland and by ship to Rio de Janeiro.[6] Mawe was given permission to visit the gold and diamond mines of Minas Gerais and other parts of the interior — the first foreigner given such an opportunity following the transfer of the Portuguese court from Lisbon to Rio and the opening of Brazilian ports to world, especially British, trade in 1808. He was also granted access to government archives.

---

6 See H.S. Torrens, 'The early life and geological work of John Mawe, 1766–1829, and a note on his travels in Brazil', *Bulletin of the Peak District Mines Historical Society*, vol. 11, no. 6, 1992, pp. 267–71.

Mawe's important book includes some excellent descriptions of the island of Santa Catarina and the adjacent mainland from where Mawe travelled to the then village of Curitiba and back to the coast at São Francisco do Sul and northwards to Santos and São Paulo. Most of the book, however, is devoted to descriptions of social and economic life in the provinces of Rio de Janeiro and of Minas Gerais, with mining (the subject of several colour illustrations) Mawe's principal interest. After his return to England in 1811 he published *Travels in the interior of Brazil* (1812), as well as *A treatise on diamonds and precious stones, including their history, natural and commercial, to which is added some account of the best methods of cutting and polishing them* (London, 1813).

PORTUGUESE TRANSLATIONS:

Lisbon, Impressão Regia, 1819, translated from the French, with many omissions and additions from other sources (only the first 208 pages were printed);

Rio de Janeiro, Livraria Editora Zélio Valverde, 1944;

Belo Horizonte and São Paulo, Editora Itatiaia/Edusp, Coleção Reconquista do Brasil, 1st série vol. 33, 1978.

Thomas Ashe, *A commercial view, and geographical sketch, of the Brasils in South America, and of the island of Madeira* (London, 1812).

Ashe was a novelist and travel writer from Ireland who 'travelled the continent of America for several years'. This book is valuable for displaying something of the excitement that infected British business interests eyeing Brazil post-1808. Approximately half of the book is devoted to English towns and cities — including Birmingham, Sheffield, Leeds, Liverpool, Nottingham, Bristol and London — and the Brazilian prospects for their shipping companies, merchants and industries. The second half of the book examines Brazilian geography, its agricultural production and describes towns, cities and captaincies, buildings and manners of men and women. Only a few pages are devoted to Madeira.

John Luccock, *Notes on Rio de Janeiro and the southern parts of Brazil taken during a residence of ten years in that country from 1808 to 1818* (London, 1820).

Luccock was a cloth merchant from Leeds importing textiles and other manufactured goods from West Yorkshire to Lisbon. In 1808 he moved to Rio de Janeiro and remained there for ten years apart from business visits back to England in 1809 and 1816[7]. Eight of the book's chapters concern Rio de Janeiro and feature detailed observations of the society and economy of both the city and the province. Four chapters are devoted to Minas Gerais (subjects ranging from the state of gold mining in the province to cruelty to animals). And two lengthy chapters record travels through the south of Brazil from Rio Grande to the island of Santa Catarina, with comments on urban life, slavery and the rural economy. The great Brazilian historian Varnhagen wrote of Luccock's book in his *História geral do Brasil* (1854–57): 'the most faithful portrayal of the material, moral and intellectual state of the capital of Brazil on the arrival of the Royal Family and of its progress during these few years'. There is a letter from Luccock to Robert Southey in November 1818 referring to his preparation of a Tupi grammar, and in an advertisement at the back of *Notes on Rio de Janeiro* Luccock announced the forthcoming publication of *Grammar and vocabulary of the Tupi language, partly collected partly translated from the works of Anchieta and Figueira noted Brazilian missionaries*. References exist to the fact that it may have been published in 1882, after Gonçalves Dias gave the manuscript to the Instituto Histórico e Geográfico Brasileiro, but this is not certain.

PORTUGUESE TRANSLATIONS:

São Paulo, Livraria Martins, Biblioteca Histórica Brasileira, 1942;

Belo Horizonte and São Paulo, Editora Itatiaia/Edusp, Coleção Reconquista do Brasil,1st série, vol. 21, 1975, based on the 1942 translation.

The chapters on Rio Grande do Sul were earlier published as *Aspectos sul-riograndenses* (Rio de Janeiro, Record, 1935).

Henry Koster, *Travels in Brazil, in the years from 1809 to 1815* (London, 1816; 2nd ed. 2 vols, 1817).

Koster, who had been born in Portugal and had grown up there, travelled from Liverpool to Pernambuco in 1809 for health reasons and remained there, apart from two return visits to England in 1811–12 and 1815–16, until his early death in 1820. He acquired a sugar *engenho* in Jaguaribe,

---

[7] See Herbert Heaton, 'A merchant adventurer in Brazil', *Journal of Economic History*, vol. 6 (1946), pp. 1–23.

land in Itamaraca and a *sítio* in Gamboa. This classic book, which Robert Southey (see p. 26) urged him to write, whose library he used and to whom it is dedicated, focuses on his experiences as a sugar planter, but other commercial and subsistence crops are discussed in some detail. In addition, there are chapters describing family and religious life in Pernambuco, the free population and slavery, public institutions and criminal activities, as well as accounts of Koster's travels to the island of Fernando de Noronha, Paraíba, Natal and Ceará. An appendix transcribes two rare pamphlets by Arruda Câmara: 'A dissertation upon the plants of Brazil from which fibrous substances may be obtained' ('Dissertação sobre as plantas do Brasil, que podem dar linhos') and 'An essay on the utility of establishing gardens in the principal provinces of Brazil for the cultivation of new plants' ('Discurso sobre a utilidade da instituição de jardins nas principais províncias do Brasil'), both originally published in Rio de Janeiro in 1810.

PORTUGUESE TRANSLATIONS:

Revista do Instituto Arqueológico e Geográfico Pernambucano, vols 51–147/150 (1898–1931) — no single volume was ever published;

São Paulo, Companhia Editora Nacional, Coleção Brasiliana vol. 221, 1942, translation and notes by Luís da Câmara Cascudo;

Recife, Fundação Joaquim Nabuco, 2002, introduction and notes by Leonardo Dantas Silva.

A.P.D.G. (anon), *Sketches of Portuguese life, manners, costume and character* (London, 1826).

In 1793, at the age of 20, the anonymous author of this work joined the Portuguese civil service, remaining so employed until 1804. He then left Portugal, but returned in 1809 with the British Army. It is not entirely clear when the author was in Brazil, although it would appear that it was sometime between 1809 and 1817. The two chapters on Brazil focus on court life in Rio de Janeiro, including accounts of musical soirées attended by castrati ('their appearance is truly disgusting') and of slavery, with observations on the importation of slaves, slave shops in the city supplying newly arrived Africans, purchasers from Minas Gerais and the supposed good treatment and 'humanity' displayed towards slaves. The author is also interested in public health and the book features a detailed account of the accumulation and manner of disposal of human waste. There are three interesting colour illustrations of Dom João VI receiving visitors, a musical soirée and a slave shop.

Archibald Campbell, *A voyage round the world, from 1806 to 1812* (Edinburgh, 1816).

Most of the journal discusses travels in Kamchatka and Alaska, but Campbell spent 22 months in Rio de Janeiro in 1810–12, where he stopped for medical treatment following the earlier amputation of both of his feet. Campbell's experiences of Rio appear to have been limited to the English and Portuguese hospitals in the city.

James Prior, *Voyage along the eastern coast of Africa, to Mosambique, Johanna, and Quiloa; to St Helena; to Rio de Janeiro, Bahia, and Pernambuco in Brazil, in the Nisus frigate* (London, 1819).

This journal (by a young Irish naval surgeon) of a voyage through the Indian and Atlantic oceans includes entries made during three months in Brazil (October 1813–January 1814). Of Rio de Janeiro, Prior remarks that 'nature and the Portuguese are at variance, for the former is all rich and magnificent, the latter poor and mean', finding the city's buildings unkept and of shoddy construction. The armed garrison is commented on, with Prior finding the men well clothed, equipped and disciplined. Women — their dress, education and morals — are discussed, as is trade with Buenos Aires and Africa. Prior stops briefly in Bahia (where he records his thoughts on the slave trade) before arriving in Pernambuco where his host is one of six resident English merchants. The towns of Pernambuco and Olinda are described and local agricultural production and foreign trade are discussed.

John Shillibeer, *A narrative of the Briton's voyage to Pitcairn's Island including an interesting sketch of the present state of the Brazils and of Spanish America* (London, 1817).

Shillibeer, a lieutenant in the Royal Marines, visited Brazil with the frigate *Briton* en route to Pitcairn Island to meet with the descendants of the *Bounty* mutineers. Although Shillibeer's stay in Rio de Janeiro was a short one (just eight days in March 1814), he goes into considerable detail in his observations of the city. The city's fortifications and port are described, as are houses, palaces, churches, theatres, markets and the 'exceedingly filthy' streets. Especially interesting are Shillibeer's many insights into slavery, describing, for example, the dead or dying lying in the streets, their owners having abandoned them to avoid funeral expenses.

There are several descriptions of Rio de Janeiro in March 1816 resulting from the visit of HMS *Alceste* transporting Lord Amherst and his party on a diplomatic mission to China:

- **Clarke Abel**, *Narrative of a journey to the interior of China, and of a voyage to and from that country, in the years 1816 and 1817* (London, 1818)

  As the official naturalist — recruited for the mission by the director of Kew Gardens, Sir Joseph Banks — Abel was especially interested in Rio de Janeiro's botanic gardens and Brazil's experimentation with tea production. But he also has interesting things to say about the accommodation offered the party in 'the best English hotel', the town's markets, slaves and their music.

- **Henry Ellis**, *Journal of the proceedings of the late embassy to China* (London, 1817; 2nd ed., 2 vols, London, 1818)

- **John McLeod**, *Voyage of His Majesty's ship Alceste* (London, 2nd ed., 1818).

Charles Waterton, *Wanderings in South America, the North-West of the United States and the Antilles, in the year 1812, 1816, 1820, and 1824* (London, 1825, and many subsequent editions).

Waterton was a traveller and naturalist with a particular interest in birds and the development of new methods of taxidermy. His book mainly recounts his extensive travels in the interior of British Guiana, but amongst other places included is an interesting account of his visit to Pernambuco in 1816. Waterton was at first not impressed with the city, finding it 'gloomy' and taken aback by the 'lamentable want of cleanliness in the streets'. He found, however, nearby places to be 'very pretty', and there are good descriptions of Monteiro and Olinda and of birdlife and fauna and flora more generally.[8]

---

8   See Alfredo de Carvalho, 'Charles Waterton em Pernambuco', *Revista do Instituto Arqueológico e Geográfico Pernambucano*, vol. XI, 1904.

William Swainson, botanist, ornithologist and ornithological illustrator, arrived in Pernambuco — the first British scientist to visit Brazil after 1808 — in December 1816, where he stayed with Henry Koster (see p. 37). Basing himself in Olinda, Swainson devoted himself to collecting birds. He also travelled to the São Francisco river and to Bahia. In April 1818 he went to Rio de Janeiro and returned from there to England four months later. Swainson's diary entries covering Brazil were published as *William Swainson, naturalist and artist: diaries 1808–1818, Sicily, Malta, Greece, Italy and Brazil* (Palmerston North, NZ, 1989), edited by Geoffrey M. Swainson.[9] Apart from ornithological-related details, the Brazil diary entries (January 1817–June 1818) include accounts concerning carnival, agriculture, slavery, punishments and prisons. Swainson also interests himself in the political situation in Brazil, especially attempted insurrections. Swainson later published *Zoological illustrations* (6 vols, London, 1820–33), *The ornithological drawings of William Swainson: Series I: The birds of Brazil* (1834), and *A selection of the birds of Brazil and Mexico* (London, 1841). Swainson is considered the best illustrator of the flora and fauna of Pernambuco, in particular since the Dutch artists resident there in the middle of the 17th century.

John Purdy, *Description of, and sailing directions for, the eastern coasts of Brasil, from Seara to Santos; including the island of Fernando Noronha* (London, 1818).

John Purdy was England's foremost authority on hydrography, producing detailed charts and guides not only to Brazil, but also to other parts of South America and the wider world. Although his guides were entirely based on secondary sources (seafarers' journals and other published books) they contain, besides detailed sailing directions, information on Brazilian ports, large and small, both regarding shipping and to assist off-duty seamen. Later editions include: *The new sailing directory for*

---

9 See also William Swainson's 'Sketch of a journey through Brazil in 1817 and 1818', *Edinburgh Philosophical Journal*, vol. 1 (June–October 1819), pp. 369–73. Swainson's Pernambuco travels are described in Alfredo de Carvalho, 'William Swainson em Pernambuco', *Revista do Instituto Arqueológico e Geográfico Pernambucano*, vol. XI, 1904, his Brazilian travels more generally in David M. Knight, 'William Swainson: naturalist, author and illustrator', *Archives of Natural History* vol. 13, no. 3 (1986) and Sheila Natusch and Geoffrey M. Swainson, *William Swainson of Fern Grove* (Wellington, NZ, 1987).

Ethiopic or southern Atlantic Ocean; including the coasts of Brasil, etc. (London, 1837); *The Brasilian navigator; or sailing directory for all the coasts of Brasil, etc.* (London, 1838; 1844). After Purdy's death in 1843, his work was carried on by Alexander George Findlay, see p. 57.

James Henderson, *A history of the Brazil; comprising its geography, commerce, colonisation, aboriginal inhabitants, etc., etc., etc.* (London, 1821).

Henderson arrived in Rio de Janeiro in 1819 hoping that Henry Chamberlain, the British consul-general, would help him to find public employment. Failing to find work, Henderson took lodgings with a British merchant in the city and undertook to at least learn what he could 'regarding the vast reaches of Brazil'. The result of Henderson's two years in Brazil was an impressive work of more than 500 pages based on his personal experience and impressions of Rio, short visits to Bahia, Pernambuco and Maranhão and what appears to be secondary information on Mato Grosso, Rio Grande do Sul and other parts of the country. It relies heavily on Ayres Casal's *Corografia Brasilica* (1817). Despite the title, the book is, like Grant's *History of Brazil* (see p. 35), more travelogue and geography than history. The subjects discussed are varied, including descriptions of houses and streets in Rio, English residents, education and slavery in that city; gauchos and cattle *fazendas* in Rio Grande do Sul; agriculture and colonisation in Santa Catarina; and the physical geography of Mato Grosso, Goiás, Bahia, Pará and Pernambuco. The book is illustrated with 28 excellent prints based on sketches produced by Henderson in the city and province of Rio de Janeiro, the varied subjects including buildings, slaves at work, militia members and means of transport.

Henry Chamberlain, *Views and costumes of the city and neighbourhood of Rio de Janeiro, Brazil, from drawings taken by Lieutenant Chamberlain, Royal Artillery, during the years 1819 and 1820, with descriptive explanations* (London, 1822).

Chamberlain, the son of the British consul-general in Rio de Janeiro, visited Brazil in 1819–20 at the age of 22. His watercolours formed the basis of a famous album of 36 lithographs, the subjects including both verdant landscapes and urban life such as means of transport, a Brazilian family, the street where slaves were sold and abandoned sick slaves. Each picture is accompanied by a detailed explanation of the particular subject.

A facsimile edition was published in Brazil: Rio de Janeiro, Livraria Kosmos Editora, Coleção Temas Brasileiros, 1943, including a TRANSLATION and introduction by Rubens Borba de Morais.

Alexander Caldcleugh, *Travels in South America during the years 1819–20-21; containing an account of the present state of Brazil, Buenos Ayres and Chile* (2 vols, London, 1825).

Caldcleugh was private secretary to the British minister in Brazil, Edward Thornton. Roughly half of the first volume relates to Brazil, mainly to the city and province of Rio de Janeiro. Caldcleugh's wide-ranging account includes descriptions of the city's houses and public buildings, its libraries, museums and markets, medical care and funerals, religion and superstition. The province's inhabitants — free, slaves and Swiss immigrants — are discussed, as are local agriculture and the city's food supply. In volume two there is a chapter on Minas Gerais, concentrating on gold mining there.

PORTUGUESE TRANSLATION: *Viagens na America do Sul. Extrato da obra contendo relato sobre o Brasil* (Belo Horizonte, Fundação João Pinheiro, 2000).

Gilbert Farquhar Mathison, *Narrative of a visit to Brazil, Chile, Peru and the Sandwich Islands during the years 1821 and 1822* (London, 1825).

Much of the book is devoted to travels in the city and province of Rio de Janeiro. Included are some early assessments of Rio's libraries, museums and theatres. Mathison, a Jamaican sugar planter, devotes two chapters to agriculture-related subjects, especially to a visit to the Swiss colony of Nova Friburgo and an account of a visit to the royal farm and residence of Santa Cruz.

MARIA GRAHAM AND BRAZIL

Maria Graham, *Journal of a voyage to Brazil and residence there, during part of the years 1821, 1822, 1823* (London, 1824).

Graham, née Dundas (the daughter of Admiral Dundas), later Lady Calcott, was the wife of Thomas Graham, a British naval officer. She visited Brazil in 1821–22 on her way to Chile on the frigate *Doris* commanded by her husband and again in 1823 on her way back to England. Her Brazilian journal — with its detailed descriptions of her surroundings and the people she encountered — is one of the best accounts of Brazil at the time of Independence.*

Maria Graham spent three weeks in Pernambuco (September–October 1821) followed by almost two months in Bahia (October–December 1821), where she was fascinated by the street life (for example, the markets and the sedan chairs carrying wealthy residents), would stop by unannounced at the homes of women acquaintances, visited, and reported on, the local hospitals and discusses the activities and attitudes of the British community. She and her husband then went to Rio de Janeiro where they remained for three months (December 1821–March 1822) before continuing their journey to Chile. Maria was widowed shortly before arriving in Valparaíso in April 1822, but she remained in Chile for almost a year. In March 1823 she returned to Brazil with Admiral Cochrane (see below, p. 46), who was travelling there to take command of the country's navy, and spent a further seven months in Rio before returning to England in October 1823.

Most of Maria Graham's *Journal* concerns Rio which Graham considered to be 'more like a European city than either Bahia or Pernambuco'. Graham comments on the dominance of the French

---

* The only biography of Maria Graham is *Maria, Lady Calcott* (London, 1937) by Rosamund Brunel Gotch, her great-great-niece. It includes a chapter on Brazil. See also Waldemar Valente, *Maria Graham — uma inglêsa em Pernambuco nos começos do século XIX* (Recife, 1957), and the introductory essay in Elizabeth Mavor, *The captain's wife. The South American journals of Maria Graham 1821–23* (London, 1993).

and English in business including both the wholesale and retail sectors, as well as in tailoring, baking and taverns. The journal also features much on the slave trade, including statistics detailing the number and source of newly arrived Africans in Rio and the treatment of slaves and the nature of their duties. Graham was also an accomplished artist with the book featuring eleven plates and nine vignettes based on pen and ink drawings that she produced in Pernambuco and Rio de Janeiro. Subjects include general landscapes and city scapes, cemeteries and slave markets, water carriers and *cadeiras*.**

PORTUGUESE TRANSLATIONS:

São Paulo, Companhia Editora Nacional, Coleção Brasiliana, Série Grande Formato, no. 8, 1956, trans. Américo Jacobina Lacombe; Belo Horizonte and São Paulo, Editora Itatiaia/Edusp, Coleção Reconquista do Brasil, nova série, vol. 157, 1990.

Waldemar Valente, *Maria Graham — uma inglêsa em Pernambuco nos começos do século XIX* (Recife, 1957) includes a PORTUGUESE TRANSLATION of the Pernambuco section of Graham's Brazilian journal.

Maria Graham again returned to Rio in 1824 at the invitation of Emperor Dom Pedro I to serve as tutor and governess to his daughter Princess Maria da Gloria (who later succeeded to the throne of Portugal after her father renounced his claims). These months are not recorded in Maria's published *Journal* (1821–23).***

** The Oliveira Lima Library at the Catholic University of America in Washington, DC has a copy of Maria Graham's *Journal* for the years 1821, 1822 and 1823 which belonged to the author and in which she had made corrections, annotations and additions, possibly for a future second edition which she never published. The annotations are particularly valuable for the insights they provide on the Confederation of the Equator and the actions of Admiral Cochrane in Pernambuco in 1824.

*** The Biblioteca Nacional in Rio has the manuscript of Graham's 1824 *Journal*. It was edited and annotated by Rodolfo Garcia and published in *Anais da Biblioteca Nacional do Rio de Janeiro*, volume LX (1938). The Biblioteca Nacional also published *Correspondência entre Maria Graham e a Imperatriz Dona Leopoldina* (Rio de Janeiro, 1940).

> On her return from Brazil to England — and before marrying the painter Sir Augustus Wall Calcott and, as Lady Calcott, spending much of the rest of her life in Italy — Maria Graham worked as a reader of travel books for the London publisher John Murray. She edited — and wrote substantial portions of — *Voyage of H.M.S. Blonde to the Sandwich Islands in the years 1824–1825* (London, 1826), said to be based on a journal kept by a Mr Bloxom (the chaplain of the *Blonde*) and that of an unidentified midshipman. The book is an account of the voyage to Honolulu of the HMS *Blonde* (under the command of Lord Byron — a cousin of the poet and grandson of Admiral Byron of the *Dolphin* — see p. 19) which was carrying the remains of the Hawaiian king, Kamehameha II, and his queen, Kamamalu, who died in London while on a visit to George IV, as well as surviving members of the couple's entourage (see also p. 47). The first part of the book recalls the royal party's outward journey to England on the *Aigle* and, as well as a short passage describing a call at the island of Santa Catarina, provides an account of the Hawaiians' three-week stay in Rio de Janeiro, including a reception by Dom Pedro I and a ball attended by 'all the principal Brazilian and English residents' and impressions formed locally of the king and queen. Returning to Hawaii, the *Blonde* called briefly at Rio, but little more is said of the city.

Thomas Cochrane, 10th Earl of Dundonald, *Narrative of services in the liberation of Chile, Peru and Brazil, from Spanish and Portuguese domination* (London, 2 vols., 1858–9).

Thomas Alexander Cochrane was a British naval officer who served in the American Revolutionary and Napoleonic Wars. He was later elected a member of Parliament (1806–16), but was expelled from both the Navy and Parliament after a stock exchange scandal. He served in the Chilean Navy (1818–22) and played a major role in the liberation of Chile and Peru from Spain. Following Brazil's declaration of Independence from Portugal in 1822 Cochrane was invited to join the Brazilian Navy — with the rank of admiral. He arrived in Rio de Janeiro in March 1823 and, after reorganising the Brazilian Navy, helped to overcome Portuguese resistance in Bahia, Pernambuco, Maranhão and Pará (August 1824–May 1825). Volume one of the *Narrative*, written towards the end of his life, is largely devoted to Chile but includes a brief account of his recruitment to command the Brazilian Navy. Volume two consists of reminiscences of his Brazilian service, with particular attention given to issues relating to pay and prize money.[10] Cochrane died in 1860.

Hugh Salvin, *Journal written on board of His Majesty's Ship Cambridge from January, 1824, to May, 1827* (Newcastle, 1829).

Salvin was the chaplain on the HMS *Cambridge* which was taking Britain's first consuls to Spanish South America (Montevideo, Buenos Aires, Valparaíso and Lima). The book includes an excellent account of the transatlantic voyage to Brazil. The *Cambridge* arrived in Rio de Janeiro in February 1824 and remained for three weeks. A meeting with Britain's consul in Rio is discussed, as is a meeting with the king of Hawaii, Kamehameha II, who was on his way to London (see also p. 46). Salvin also describes Rio life generally, including interesting observations on English merchants and African slaves.

Brazilian Improvements, more particularly as regards the province of Espirito Santo (London, 1825), 'By a well-wisher to Brazilian Independence', is an account of the supposedly excellent trading and investment opportunities awaiting British merchants in Espírito Santo. The publication offers useful information on a usually overlooked part of Brazil and is valuable not least for its account of the province's Indian inhabitants.

Josiah Conder, *The modern traveller. A popular description, geographical, historical, and topographical, of the various countries of the globe. Brazil and Buenos Ayres* (2 vols, London, 1825).

In 1824, bookseller and author Josiah Conder entered into an agreement to edit what was to become a very well-known series of books, *The*

---

10 There are several biographies of Cochrane, all of which include chapters on his service with the Brazilian Navy. See Christopher Lloyd, *Lord Cochrane* (London, 1947); Ian Grimble, *The sea wolf. The life of Admiral Lord Cochrane* (London, 1978); and Robert Harvey, *Cochrane. The life and exploits of a fighting captain* (London, 2000), which also discusses the admiral's relationship with Maria Graham (see p. 44).

modern traveller. Following the success of the first volume (Palestine), Conder went on to edit some thirty other volumes (1825–29), including two on Brazil. The pocket books are a compilation of extracts from British and other authors, with the Brazilian volumes including extracts from the work of Southey (see p. 26), Graham (see p. 44), Koster (see p. 37) and others. Following chapters on the geography and history of Brazil, chapters are arranged province-by-province.

John Macdouall, *Narrative of a voyage to Patagonia and Tierra del Fuego* (London, 1833).

It would appear that Macdouall was a Scottish medical officer serving with the HMS *Beagle* and HMS *Adventurer* under the command of Captain Pringle Stokes on their voyage to survey the coastline of southern South America in 1826–27. This is by far the best of the records of these ships' Brazilian ports of call and of the crew members' overland excursions; over one third of the book records Macdouall's impressions of Rio de Janeiro (including excellent accounts of the 1826 rebellion of Irish and German mercenaries and of slave dealing), São Paulo, Santos, Paranaguá and the island of Santa Catarina.

Robert FitzRoy, ed., *Narrative of the surveying voyages of His Majesty's Ships Adventurer and Beagle between the years 1826 and 1836* (3 vols, London, 1839).

FitzRoy was a hydrographer and a meteorologist best known for his association with Charles Darwin. In 1827 he sailed to South America to join the *Adventurer* and *Beagle*, taking command of the ships following the suicide of Captain Stokes. Volume one of FitzRoy's *Narrative* includes a passing mention of calling at Rio de Janeiro in 1828 (but also including a fine Augustus Earle print of the port area and cathedral) and a brief mention of landing on the island of Santa Catarina. In volume two he records his impressions of Cabo Frio and especially of Rio de Janeiro in 1830. He was appalled by the city's narrow streets, 'offensive sights and smells', 'naked negroes', and 'uncivil and ill-looking native population'. Volume three of the *Narrative* is credited to Darwin (see p. 52).[11]

---

11 See two recent biographies of Fitzroy, John and Mary Gribbin, *Fitzroy* (London, 2003) and Peter Nichols, *Evolution's captain* (London, 2003).

Henry Lister Maw, *Journal of a passage from the Pacific to the Atlantic, crossing the Andes in the northern provinces of Peru, and descending the River Marañon, or Amazon* (London, 1829).

Maw, a Royal Navy lieutenant, was a member of a team in 1828 investigating the practicality of opening a land and river trading route to link Lima and the Atlantic. Over half the book records Maw's travels through Brazil, with chapters on Tabitinga on the Peruvian border, the people he encountered (including Indian tribes and British communities), agricultural production, trade and shipping in towns along the Amazon including Egas, Obidos, Manaus, Santarém and Pará.

PORTUGUESE TRANSLATION: Liverpool, 1831, trans. António Julião da Costa, Portuguese consul in Liverpool.

William Henry Bayley Webster, *Narrative of a voyage to the Southern Atlantic Ocean in 1828, 29, 30, performed in the H.M. sloop Chanticleer* (2 vols, London, 1834).

Webster was a scientist and medical officer with the *Chanticleer*, the principal object of its mission being 'to ascertain the true figure of the earth by a series of pendulum experiments at various places in the northern and southern hemispheres'. Heading south to Antarctica — he was the first scientist to spend as long as a year there — and again northward bound to the Caribbean, the *Chanticleer* called at Brazilian ports, visits that Webster recorded in great detail. Volume one of the *Narrative* includes an account of a twelve-day call at Rio de Janeiro in July 1828. Webster pays particular attention to the city's water supply and sewage, churches, schools, bookshops, museums, hotels and the botanic gardens. Trade (mainly the export of coffee) is discussed at length. Webster's impressions of slavery and slaves are especially vivid. Six days in Santa Catarina — 'the garden of Brazil' — are also recalled, with descriptions of the island's landscape, settlements, agriculture and fishing.

Volume two features an excellent chapter on a six-day stay on Fernando de Noronha in 1830, with descriptions of the island's landscape and vegetation, the military garrison and village, fishing, cattle and the attempts at growing cotton and corn. There are two chapters detailing Webster's six weeks in the city of Maranhão (São Luís), providing invaluable insights into life and manners, especially regarding women and domestic slaves, as well as interesting descriptions of the city generally, its port area, medical facilities and convents. Pará is also described, with observations on slavery and education of particular interest.

James Holman, *A voyage round the world, including travels in Africa, Asia, Australasia, America, etc., etc., from 1828 to 1832* (4 vols, London, 1834; 2nd ed. *Travels in Brazil, Cape Colony etc*, London, 1840).

Holman entered the British Navy in 1798 at the age of twelve, but was invalided out in 1810. By the time he was 25 he had completely lost his sight. He went on to become a prolific author, visiting Europe, Africa and South America and became known as 'the blind traveller'. In 1828, Holman set off on a voyage around the world. After lengthy stays in the Atlantic islands and West Africa, he arrived in Rio de Janeiro in August 1829. Two short chapters in volume one and three short chapters in volume two, in the form of short diary entries, are devoted to Brazil, where he remained for about two months. Holman was especially interested in the activities of the Imperial British Brazilian Mining Company. A journey by mule and foot to the company's mines at Gongo Soco, near Ouro Preto, where he encountered Cornish miners and black slaves, is described at length.

Rev. Robert Walsh, *Notices of Brazil in 1828 and 1829* (2 vols, London 1830).

Walsh, an Irish Anglican clergyman and author of books on Dublin and Constantinople, was chaplain to the British mission in Rio de Janeiro, 1828–31. Volume one is a mix of historical accounts, natural history and, especially, short personal observations. Walsh describes Rio's churches, nuns and nunneries and discusses slavery, black soldiers in the Brazilian army, the conflict with Buenos Aires, medical care, education and Lancasterian schools, trade and food supply. He also investigates the 1826 insurrection of Irish and German mercenaries. Volume two includes accounts of travels into the interior of Rio de Janeiro and to Minas Gerais, with the focus on mining, and observations on slavery.

PORTUGUESE TRANSLATION: Belo Horizonte and São Paulo, Editora Itatiaia/ Edusp, Coleção Reconquista do Brasil, nova série, vols 74–75, 1985.

ARMITAGE'S HISTORY OF BRAZIL

John Armitage, *The history of Brazil, from the period of the arrival of the Braganza family in 1808 to the abdication of Dom Pedro the First in 1831, compiled from state documents and other original sources* (2 vols, London, 1836).

Planned as a sequel to Southey's *History* (see pp. 26–28), this was the first detailed history of the period 1808–31, including Brazil's Independence from Portugal and the abdication of Brazil's first emperor, Dom Pedro I. Like Southey's *History* it was based on primary sources, but unlike Southey's *History* it was also based on first hand knowledge of the country.

John Armitage spent eight years' residence in Brazil as a merchant. He arrived, aged 21, in 1828 and soon became a close friend of Evaristo da Veiga, the journalist and politician, editor and publisher (since 1827) of the most influential liberal newspaper of the period, the *Aurora Fluminense*. Evaristo introduced him to many of Brazil's leading intellectuals and politicians. He was one of the few foreigners to belong to the Rio de Janeiro branch of the Sociedade Defensora da Liberdade e Independencia, established in 1831 on Masonic lines, to which most liberal politicians and their more influential supporters were affiliated. Evaristo was also a bookseller and book collector, and just as Southey had used the Rev. Herbert Hills' library, Armitage made good and frequent use of that belonging to Evaristo da Veiga. Armitage's *History of Brazil*, which has even been credited to Evaristo by some commentators, remained a fundamental text for all later historians of the period, for example, Octávio Tarquínio de Sousa, author of *História dos fundadores do Império do Brasil* (10 vols, 1957–58).

Armitage returned to England in 1835. After the publication of his book he spent twenty years in Ceylon, where he died in 1856.

> PORTUGUESE TRANSLATIONS:
>
> Rio de Janeiro, Typographia de J. Villeneuve, 1837, translation by Joaquim Teixeira de Macedo (sometimes erroneously credited to Evaristo da Veiga).
>
> Later editions all based on the Teixeira de Macedo translation:
>
> Rio de Janeiro, 1914, with notes by Eugenio Egas;
>
> Rio de Janeiro, Livraria Editora Zélio Valverde, 1943, with notes by Eugenio Egas and Garcia Júnior;
>
> São Paulo, Martins, 1972;
>
> São Paulo, Editora Melhoramentos, 1977;
>
> Belo Horizonte and São Paulo, Editora Itatiaia/Edusp, Coleção Reconquista do Brasil, nova série, vol. 45, 1981.
>
> There is no modern critical edition of Armitage's *History of Brazil* in English or Portuguese.

1831–1870

Charles Darwin, *Journals and remarks 1832–6*, the final volume of the three-volume *Narrative of the surveying voyages of His Majesty's Ships 'Adventure' and 'Beagle' between the years 1826 and 1836* (London, 1839), edited by Captain Robert FitzRoy (see p. 48), published separately as *Journal of researches into the natural history and geology of the various countries visited by H.M.S. Beagle* (London, 1839), and in numerous MODERN EDITIONS as *The voyage of the Beagle*.

Darwin was twice in Brazil during the second voyage of HMS *Beagle* (December 1831– October 1836): first in Bahia in February 1832 (just 23 years old and horrified by the slave society he encountered there) and Rio de Janeiro in April–June, from where he sent home by naval vessel consignments of carefully labelled specimens; and again, very briefly, in Bahia and Recife on the return journey in August 1836. The references to Rio in his diary and correspondence include an account of an excursion to Cabo Frio, thoughts on slavery (including notes concerning a *quilombo*) and observations on meteorology and entomology.[12]

PORTUGUESE TRANSLATION: *Viagem de um naturalista ao redor do mundo*, Rio de Janeiro, Companhia Brasil Editora, 1937.

Charles James Fox Bunbury, *Life, letters and journals of Sir Charles James Fox Bunbury* (edited by his wife, Frances Joanna Bunbury, 3 vols, London 1894; another edition edited by his sister-in-law, Mrs Henry Lyell, 2 vols, London, 1906).

Bunbury, a botanist, was in Brazil in 1833–35. Volume one includes some of his letters and journal entries written in Rio de Janeiro and Minas Gerais concerning trade, slaves, expedition costs, plants, mines and minerals.

Bunbury's unpublished journal 'An account of a journey in Brazil in 1833–5' was published in PORTUGUESE TRANSLATION: 'Narrativa de viagem de um naturalista inglês ao Rio de Janeiro e Minas Gerais, 1833–35', *Anais da Biblioteca Nacional no Rio de Janeiro*, vol. LXII (1940), and later by Editora Itatiaia/Edusp, Coleção Reconquista do Brasil, nova série, vol. 31, 1981.

John Gould, *A monograph of the Ramphastidae or family of toucans* (London, 1834).

Gould was a taxidermist and an extremely successful ornithological illustrator. His large-format book on toucans includes dozens of stunning full-colour illustrations, all accompanied by text describing their bone structure, feathering and natural habitat. Many of the toucans featured

---

12 There are innumerable editions of Darwin's correspondence and diaries, but with only limited reference to Brazil. See Nora Barlow, ed., *Diary of the Voyage of H.M.S. Beagle* (London, 1933); Fredrick Burckhardt, ed., *The correspondence of Charles Darwin, 1821–36* (Cambridge, 1985); Richard Darwin Keynes, *The Beagle record: selections from the original pictoral records and written accounts of the voyage of H.M.S. Beagle* (Cambridge, 1979); Richard Darwin Keynes, ed., *Charles Darwin's Beagle diary* (Cambridge 1988). See also Adrian Desmond and James Moore, *Darwin* (London, 1992); Janet Browne, *Charles Darwin*. Vol. I *Voyaging* (London and New York, 1995); Keith S. Thomson, *HMS Beagle. The ship that changed the course of history* (New York, 1995); and Richard Darwin Keynes, *Fossils, finches and Fuegians: Charles Darwin's adventures and discoveries on the Beagle, 1832–1836* (London, 2002).

in the book are species native to Brazil, but Gould never visited South America, basing his illustrations entirely on the examination of the stuffed birds held in British and other European ornithological collections.

Lieut. William Smyth and **Frederick Lowe**, *Narrative of a journey from Lima to Para across the Andes and down the Amazon* (London, 1836).

The final two chapters follow the expedition through Brazil from the Peruvian border at Tabitinga, down the Amazon and then the Rio Negro to investigate the practicality of commercial navigation linking the Atlantic with the Amazon region. There are some good descriptions of Amazon basin settlements, especially Santarém, with observations on the Indian population and local economic activities.

Peter Campbell Scarlett, *South America and the Pacific; comprising a journey across the Pampas and the Andes* (2 vols, London, 1838).

Scarlett was a diplomat who arrived in Rio de Janeiro in September 1834 to take up a position of attaché at the British Legation. In addition to three chapters with a detailed account of the transatlantic voyage, Scarlett offers his first impressions of Rio in one chapter of volume one. Scarlett was a guest of William Gore Ousely, the secretary of the British Legation, and he describes his house in Botafogo. Scarlett's work is not discussed, but his social life is, such as attending a ball given by the Russian consul-general, noting that 'ices were served, being the first introduction of the luxury into the Brazils, in consequence of the arrival of a cargo of ice from Boston'. The 'hideous' condition of slaves is described in some detail, with Scarlett expressing shock at how their appearance is 'of a more loathsome object than any other animal'. There is also an account of a visit by Scarlett to the Visconde do Santo Amaro's sugar estate near Rio. After only a few weeks in Rio, Scarlett left Brazil to travel elsewhere in South America.

Alexander Paton, *Narrative of the loss of the shooner Clio of Montrose, Captain George Reid, containing an account of the massacre of her crew by the Indians on the north coast of Brazil in October 1835* (London, 1838; 3rd edition, Montrose, 1879).

Paton, a young sailor from the Scottish fishing village of Ferryden, was the sole survivor of a schooner carrying cargo from Liverpool to Pará which ran aground in a remote spot northwest of Maranhão. Paton recounts the wreck itself, the massacre by Indians of the other six crew members and being sheltered by a Catholic priest. The measured language and the landmarks indicated help to make the account entirely believable.

George Gardner, *Travels in the interior of Brazil principally through the northern provinces and the gold mining districts during the years 1836–41* (London, 1846, 2nd edition 1849).

Encouraged by his former professor at Glasgow University, William Hooker (a future director of Kew Gardens), Gardner went to Brazil in 1836 to collect botanical specimens, travelling widely in southeastern, central and northeastern parts of the country. This extremely important record of Gardner's travels (including Rio de Janeiro, Bahia, Pernambuco, Ceará, Alagoas, Piauí and Minas Gerais), does not only concern the natural history of the places that he visited. Wherever he is, Gardner records his impressions of the local economy and society, discussing sugar plantations in Ceará, slavery ('very few [slaves] expressed any regret at having been taken from their own countries') in Rio de Janeiro, mining in Diamantina and Ouro Preto, German immigrants in the interior of Pernambuco and Swiss immigrants in Nova Friburgo. In 1844 Gardner was appointed superintendent of the Royal Botanical Gardens of Ceylon and he prepared his Brazilian journals for publication during the long voyage east.

PORTUGUESE TRANSLATIONS:

São Paulo, Companhia Editora Nacional, Coleção Brasiliana vol. 223, 1942, trans. Albertino Pinheiro;

Belo Horizonte and São Paulo, Editora Itatiaia/Edusp, Coleção Reconquista do Brasil, 1st série, vol. 13, 1975.

Richard Schomburgk, *Reissen in Britisch Guiana* (3 vols, Leipzig, 1847–48; English-language edition, Georgetown, 1922).

Robert Schomburgk, a German-born, British naturalised failed West Indian tobacco planter was commissioned in 1834 by the Royal Geographical Society to explore the far south of British Guiana. In 1840 he was commissioned to make a survey of the colony's boundaries, and for this he was accompanied by his brother, Richard, who became a naturalised British subject in 1849. Richard's book includes material on the British Guiana–Brazil border region, but it is considered most reliable on botanical matters. Although Robert did not himself produce a book based on his travels, he contributed numerous important articles to the *Journal of the Royal Geographical Society*.[13]

Alexander George Findlay, *The Brasilian navigator or sailing directory for all the coasts of Brasil* (London, 1851).

Findlay, a Fellow of the Royal Geographical Society, drew chiefly on the work of John Purdy (see p. 41). There were numerous later editions: e.g. *A sailing directory for the coasts of Brasil* (London, 1882).

Sir William Gore Ouseley, *Views in South America, from original drawings made in Brazil, the River Plate, the Parana, etc.* (London, 1852); *Description of views in South America, from original drawings made in Brazil, the River Plate, the Parana, etc.* (London, 1852).

Ouseley, the eldest son of the eminent Orientalist Sir William Ouseley, went to Rio de Janeiro in 1832 as secretary of the British Legation and was appointed chargé-d'affaires in 1838. In 1844 he moved to Buenos Aires following his appointment as British minister to the Argentine Republic, and returned to England in 1850. An accomplished artist, a selection of his paintings was reproduced as colour lithographs and published in an album, with detailed background information regarding each of them in a companion volume. The album features 27 lithographs, including five scenes of Bahia and fifteen of Rio de Janeiro, both of churches and other buildings in these cities, and of scenes of the countryside and villages nearby.

PORTUGUESE TRANSLATION: in Affonso de E. Taunay, *Rio de Janeiro de antanho* (São Paulo, Companhia Editora Nacional, 1942).

Robert Dundas, *Sketches of Brazil, including new views on tropical and European fever* (London, 1852).

Dundas was for 23 years (1819–42) the medical supervisor at the British hospital in Salvador (Bahia). The book, based on lectures that he gave

---

13 See Peter Rivière, *Absent-minded imperialism: Britain and the expansion of empire in nineteenth-century Brazil* (London, 1995) for an account of how the border between Brazil and British Guiana came to be drawn.

at the Northern Hospital in Liverpool, reflects Dundas' interest in tropical medicine, outlining the symptoms and treatment of illnesses both common and unusual in Bahia at the time, the supposed importance of climate for the transmission of infection and the physical and moral conditions of the population. The British hospital in Salvador is described and the training of doctors both there and in Rio de Janeiro is discussed.

Fred Walpole, *Four years in the Pacific in her Majesty's ship Collingwood from 1844 to 1848* (2 vols, London, 1849; 2nd ed., London, 1850).

Walpole was a lieutenant in the Royal Navy, whose Pacific-bound ship called at Rio de Janeiro in 1844. Two chapters relate to Brazil, one of which is essentially a general history of the country, the other concerns Rio. The immense difficulty of landing at the port is recounted and the incredible filth of the area around the docks. The slave market — 'a miserable hole' — is described in some detail, especially the floggings and the sale of babies.

WALLACE, BATES AND SPRUCE IN AMAZONIA

The letters, journals and books of the three great British naturalists who contributed so much to the exploration and scientific discovery of the Amazon in the middle decades of the 19th century — **Alfred Russel Wallace**, co-founder with Darwin of the theory of evolution by natural selection, **Henry Walter Bates** and **Richard Spruce** — are especially important for our knowledge and understanding of Brazil.

Wallace and Bates, aged 25 and 23 respectively, inspired by the book *A voyage up the river Amazon* (New York, 1846), by the American travel writer William H. Edwards, travelled to Pará in 1848 intending to collect entomological specimens for private dealers and for Kew Gardens, which had been reorganised in 1841 and formally recognised as the national botanic garden under the direction of Sir William Hooker (and later his son Sir Joseph Hooker). They remained together for two years on the lower Amazon between Belém and Santarém, parting company in 1850.

Wallace spent two more years on the Rio Negro and the Orinoco, while Bates remained another nine years on the Solimões and Upper Amazon.

Returning to England in 1852 on the ill-fated brig *Helen* Wallace lost most of his notes, sketches and, worst of all, his collections in a shipboard fire, but nevertheless published the following year *A narrative of travels on the Amazon and Rio Negro* (London, 1853; 2nd edition 1889). As an appendix to the volume he included notes on the natural history, geography and geology of the Amazon valley and its aboriginal tribes, with vocabularies of Amazonian languages, which represent a mere fragment of the *Physical history of the Amazon* he had planned to write.*

PORTUGUESE TRANSLATIONS: São Paulo, Companhia Editora Nacional, Brasiliana vol. 156, 1939; Belo Horizonte and São Paulo, Editora Itatiaia/Edusp, Coleção Reconquista do Brasil, 1st série, vol. 50, 1979.

Other Brazil-related books by Wallace are *Palm trees of the Amazon and their uses* (London, 1853) and his autobiography, *My life. A record of events and opinions* (2 vols, London, 1905).

Henry Bates was encouraged by Darwin to write his classic *A naturalist on the River Amazon; a record of adventures, habits of animals, sketches of Brazilian and Indian life, and aspects of nature under the Equator* (2 vols, London, 1863 and numerous later editions) after his return to England in 1859. After eleven years in Amazonia, he was, Darwin believed, second only to Humboldt in his knowledge of tropical forests. He regarded the book as 'the best book of natural history travels ever published in England'. Bates recounts in great detail his work, travels and

---

*See Barbara G. Beddall, *Wallace and Bates in the tropics* (London, 1969); Sandra Knapp, *Footsteps in the forests: Alfred Russel Wallace in the Amazon* (London, Natural History Museum, 1999); Peter Raby, *Alfred Russel Wallace. A life* (London, 2001); *Infinite tropics. An Alfred Russel Wallace anthology*, ed. Andrew Berry (London, 2001); Michael Shermer, *In Darwin's shadow. The life and science of Alfred Russel Wallace* (Oxford, 2002).

adventure in the Brazilian Amazon, describing means of travel, plants, insects and animals that he collected or examined and the lives of local officials, cattle or cocoa farmers, Indians and other people he worked with or encountered. Bates became for thirty years the first (paid) secretary of the Royal Geographical Society which had been founded in the 1830s.**

PORTUGUESE TRANSLATIONS: São Paulo, Companhia Editora Nacional, Brasiliana vol. 237, 1944; Belo Horizonte and São Paulo, Editora Itatiaia/Edusp, Coleção Reconquista do Brasil, 1st série, vol. 53, 1979.

Wallace and Bates were primarily entomologists, Richard Spruce a botanist (though all three, it should be said, were also explorers, geographers, geologists, anthropologists, linguists and much else besides). Spruce (aged 32, though with an established reputation for his work in Yorkshire and the Pyrenees) went to the Amazon in 1849, a year after Wallace and Bates. He stayed in northern Brazil, Peru and Ecuador for fifteen years — until 1864. On his return he published P*almae Amazonicae* (London, 1869) and later his monumental *Hepaticae Amazonicae et Andinae* (1884–85). Fifteen years after his death his friend Wallace collected and edited his *Notes of a botanist on the Amazon and the Andes* (2 vols, 1908).***

A fourth British scientific explorer William Chandless visited Amazonia in 1861, 1864–65 and 1866. He never wrote a book, but contributed an important series of articles to the *Journal of the Royal Geographical Society*.

** See Beddall, *Wallace and Bates in the tropics*, op.cit.; George Woodcock, *H.W. Bates, naturalist of the Amazons* (London, 1969). Also John Dickenson, 'Bates, Wallace and economic botany in mid nineteenth century Amazonia', in M.R.D. Seaward and S.M.D. Fitzgerald, eds, *Richard Spruce (1817–1893). Botanist and explorer* (London, Royal Botanic Gardens, Kew, 1996) and 'H.W. Bates — the naturalist of the River Amazon', *Archives of Natural History*, vol. 19 (1992).
*** See Victor W. Von Hagen, *South America called them* (London, 1949); Seaward and Fitzgerald, eds, *Richard Spruce (1817–1893)*, op.cit.; Mark R.D. Seaward, 'Richard Spruce, botánico e desbravador da América do Sul', *Historia, Ciencias, Saude. Manguinhos*, vol. 7, no. 2 (2000).

Alexander Marjoribanks, *Travels in South and North America* (Edinburgh, 1852; London, 1853).

This is an account of travels between Australia and Canada, via the Falkland Islands, Brazil and the United States in 1850–52. Four lengthy chapters are devoted to Brazil with descriptions of Bahia and Rio de Janeiro, especially in relation to the British and other foreign mercantile communities in those cities, marriage and the position of women, religion and the Catholic Church. Slavery and the slave trade receives particular attention with the number and source of new arrivals from Africa given and some questioning as to the wisdom of pushing ahead with slave emancipation.

John Candler and **Wilson Burgess**, *Narrative of a recent visit to Brazil* (London, 1853).

Burgess and Chandler visited Brazil in 1852 to collect information for the Religious Society of Friends (the Quakers) concerning slavery and the slave trade. The authors travelled widely and there are chapters on Pernambuco, Rio de Janeiro (where they met the emperor, the British minister and English Quakers), Petrópolis, Minas Gerais (relating a visit to the St John d'El Rey gold mines), Vitória, Bahia and Maceió.

William Hadfield, *Brazil, the River Plate, and the Falkland Islands* (London, 1854).

Hadfield was secretary of the South American and General Steam Navigation Company. The book is both a history of the region, a guidebook and a travelogue recounting personal impressions of a visit in 1853. Although most of Brazil's provinces are discussed, only the entries for Pernambuco, Bahia and Rio de Janeiro appear to be based on first hand observations. The book is accompanied by illustrations from William Gore Ouseley's *Views in South America* (see p. 56). There are later editions of this work: *Brazil and the River Plate in 1868, showing the progress of those countries since the author's former visit in 1853* (London, 1869) and *Brazil and the River Plate 1870–76* (London, 1877).

Edward Wilberforce, *Brazil viewed through a naval glass: with notes on slavery and the slave trade* (London, 1855).

Wilberforce (a grandson of William Wilberforce, the anti-slavery campaigner) records somewhat randomly impressions of Rio de Janeiro (both the city, Mangaratiba and Ilha Grande), Santos, Espírito Santo and Salvador, describing the local landscapes and economies, diet, shops, trade and slavery. Wilberforce was an officer on a British warship on anti-slave trade patrol. It is not clear from the text when he actually visited Brazil.

Charles Blachford Mansfield, *Paraguay, Brazil, and the Plate. Letters written 1852–1853* (Cambridge, 1856).

Mansfield was a distinguished chemist who visited Brazil in 1852–53. The book is based on letters collected and published posthumously. (Mansfield died following a fire in his Cambridge laboratory in 1855.) It includes letters from Pernambuco and Rio de Janeiro. Mansfield was immediately impressed by Brazil: 'what a Paradise is, or at least might be, this country if it were possessed by the English!'. He offers his impressions of black Brazilians ('splendid specimens of muscular development'), English residents, sugar and coffee production and the natural history of the places he visited.

James Wetherell, *Brazil. Stray notes from Bahia: being extracts from letters etc. during a residence of fifteen years* (Liverpool, 1860).

Wetherell went to Bahia in 1842 and soon after found employment in the British consulate there. The book consists of a series of notes, arranged by year, on topics of local interest that caught Wetherell's imagination such as African princes in the city, musical instruments, food, etiquette and clothing. Wetherell left Bahia in 1857 when he was appointed vice-consul in Paraíba. He died in 1858, at the age of 36, following a fall. The book was compiled posthumously by friends and edited by William Hadfield.

PORTUGUESE TRANSLATION: *Apontamentos sobre a Bahia, 1842–57* (Salvador, Banco da Bahia, 1972).

Robert Elwes, *A sketcher's tour round the world* (London, 1854).

Elwes records in some detail his visit to Rio de Janeiro in 1848. Unusually for a British visitor, he found that the narrowness of the city's streets served a useful purpose, 'affording protection from the scorching sun' and was impressed by the system of one-way streets. He commented on the shopkeepers: most were French, some Portuguese or Brazilian, and some (the worst) English. Slavery in the city and the slave trade are discussed as is the position of German and Swiss immigrants whom he observes when visiting Petrópolis. Elwes also travels by land to Bahia, with most of this section of the book recording events relating to the interception of Brazilian slavers by British warships.

Hamlet Clark, *Letters home from Spain, Algeria, and Brazil, during past entomological rambles* (London, 1867).

The author travelled to Brazil in 1856–57, briefly visiting Pernambuco and Bahia but spending most time in the city and province of Rio de Janeiro to which over a third of the book is devoted. Some of the content of the letters details the observation and collection of insects, but Clark mainly decribes his travels. He generally formed a very favourable impression of Brazil, especially its scenery which is described in detail. His only dislike was slavery, mainly because he was not impressed by the enslaved. Clark's travelling companion was an artist John Gray, who contributed several colour lithographs to the book depicting lush vegetation of the interior of Brazil and the houses where they stayed.

Fenton Aylmer, *A cruise in the Pacific. From the log of a naval officer* (2 vols, London 1860).

Included in volume one is a chapter surveying Brazilian history and another chapter recording Captain Aylmer's visit to Rio de Janeiro in the late 1850s. Besides general impressions of the city he describes visits to the Corcovado and the botanical gardens.

Thomas Woodbine Hinchliff, *South American sketches; or a visit to Rio de Janeiro, the Organ Mountains, La Plata and the Paraná* (London, 1863).

Hinchliff's Brazilian travels mainly took him through the province of Rio de Janeiro, but he also briefly visited Juiz da Fora in Minas Gerais, Pernambuco and Bahia. The city of Rio de Janeiro, Petrópolis and Teresópolis are especially well described, with particular attention to hotels in which the author stayed, the condition of roads and railways and the labour question, both regarding slaves and immigrants.

A second journey in 1873 is described in *Over the sea and far away, being a narrative of wanderings around the world* (London, 1876).

William Dougal Christie, *Notes on Brazilian questions* (London, 1865).

Christie was British minister from 1859 to 1863 and the cause of one of the most famous diplomatic incidents in Brazilian history (the 'Christie affair') that came about when, following a number of 'incidents' involving British naval officers and seamen, he ordered in December 1862 the blockade of the port of Rio de Janeiro and the seizure by British ships of several Brazilian vessels that were believed to be trading in slaves (more than ten years after the trade had been, it was thought, finally brought to an end). This led to the suspension of British–Brazilian diplomatic relations, which were not restored until July 1865. This important book deals with this and many other 'Brazilian questions' of the time, including slavery, abolition, commercial relations with Britain, and Brazilian policy in the Río de la Plata.

William Scully, *Brazil; its provinces and chief cities; the manners and customs of the people; agricultural, commercial and other statistics, taken from the latest official documents and a variety of useful and entertaining knowledge, both for the merchant and emigrant* (London, 1866; 2nd ed., 1868).

Scully was the Irish-born proprietor and editor of the *Anglo-Brazilian Times*, a newspaper published in Rio de Janeiro from February 1865 to 1884. His book was essentially a prospectus for investors and a guidebook for British, and especially Irish, immigrants. The book includes a province-by-province assessment of Brazil's prospects and features chapters on history, manners and customs, and trade. There are several useful tables.

L. Dillon, *A twelve months' tour in Brazil and the River Plate* (Manchester, 1867).

This book is based on a series of letters that Dillon sent to his father in Buxton, Derbyshire, while travelling to, and in, South America to assess sheep farming prospects there. He was not impressed by either Pernambuco or Bahia and worried a good deal about the effects of the local food. In Rio de Janeiro he appreciated the 'luxuriance of the tropical vegetation, and the variety of the flowers and trees nothing short of enrapturing', but otherwise remained unimpressed by the city due to its narrow streets, poor pavements and 'wretched smells'.

Robert O. Cunningham, *Notes on the natural history of the Strait of Magallan and the west coast of Patagonia* (Edinburgh, 1871).

Cunningham served as the naturalist with HMS *Nassau*, a small steamer sent to survey the Strait of Magellan. The ship called at Rio de Janeiro three times between 1866 and 1869 and separate chapters of the book are devoted to each of the visits. Cunningham is especially interested in matters relating to Rio de Janeiro's natural history, but also discussed are the city's parks, the Dom Pedro railway and the general way of life.

John Hale Murray, *Travels in Uruguay, South America* (London, 1871).

In 1868 Murray travelled from England to Uruguay to take up the position of Anglican chaplain in Colonia. The book includes an excellent description of the transatlantic voyage, followed by brief accounts of calls at Pernambuco, Bahia and Rio de Janeiro. In each place he showed particular interest in the physical appearance of the population, especially the black population. Included in the account of his stay in Rio de Janeiro is a detailed description of a fifty-person slave gang engaged in the re-coaling of the steamer in which he was travelling as well as descriptions of an excursion to Tijuca and of the botanical gardens.

Arthur Drummond Carlisle, *Round the world in 1870. An account of a brief tour through India, China, Japan, California, and South America* (London, 1872).

Carlisle spent the entire year of 1870 travelling around the world. Rio de Janeiro was one of his final ports of call, to which he devotes one short chapter of the book. He contrasts Rio de Janeiro's architecture and inhabitants with those of Buenos Aires and Montevideo and provides good descriptions of Rio's mule-drawn trams and of slaves being hired out as day labourers. He also provides a brief account of a visit to Petrópolis, which he describes as 'a Brazilian Balmoral'.

BURTON IN BRAZIL AND PARAGUAY

Sir Richard Burton, the great 'orientalist' and explorer, was British consul in Santos 1865–68. He was appointed in July 1864, embarked in May 1865 and, after a few months in Recife, arrived in September 1865. It was for him a dreary position but one which allowed some travel opportunities and sufficient leisure for his translations. *Explorations of the highlands of Brazil, with a full account of the gold and diamond mines, also canoeing down 1500 miles of the Great River São Francisco from Sabará to the sea* (2 vols, 1869) contains extensive material on mining in Minas Gerais (Burton's justification for receiving leave from his consular position which enabled him to embark on his travels in 1867) and an account of his descent of the São Francisco River ('Brazil's Mississippi') through Minas Gerais and Pernambuco to the Atlantic Ocean at Maceió, as well as strong criticism of the Catholic Church, which he hated.

PORTUGUESE TRANSLATIONS:

Viagens aos planaltos do Brasil (1868), trans. Américo Jacobina Lacombe. Vol. I. *Do Rio de Janeiro a Morro Velho* (São Paulo, Companhia Editora Nacional, Coleção Brasiliana vol. 197, 1941, 2nd ed., 1983); vol. II *Minas e os mineiros*, vol. III *O Rio São Francisco*, Coleção Brasiliana, vols 375–6, 1983;

Belo Horizonte and São Paulo, Editora Itatiaia/Edusp, Coleção Reconquista do Brasil, 1st série, vol. 36 *Viagem do Rio de Janeiro a Morro Velho*, 1976; vol. 37 *Viagem de Canoa de Sabará ao o Oceano Atlântico*, 1977.

Volume I of *The life of Captain Sir Richard F. Burton* (2 vols, London, 1893) by **Isabel Burton**, Sir Richard's wife, a devout Catholic, includes a chapter on the Burtons' three years in Brazil, covering life in Santos and São Paulo, still a sleepy provincial town, and their travels. Lady Burton's autobiography, *The romance of Isabel Lady Burton* (London, 1897) was completed after her death by **William Henry Wilkins**. Included are four chapters on the Burtons' years in Brazil. Especially interesting are the letters that are reproduced, with fine descriptions of Santos and elsewhere in Brazil.

Apart from travel, Burton's other great passion was translation, with Portuguese, which he learned in Goa, his favourite language after Arabic. While in Brazil Burton, besides beginning his masterpiece *Arabian Nights* (published in 1885) and a translation of Camões' *Lusiads* (published in 1880), translated several Brazilian works: Francisco José Maria de Lacerda's *Lands of the Cazembe* (London, 1873), an account of the Brazilian explorer's travels in East Africa at the end of the 18th century — the annotations alone forming almost half the book; two contemporary novels: J.M. Pereira da Silva's *Manuel de Moraes. A chronicle of the 17th century* (London, 1886) and José de Alencar's *Iracema. The Honey-Lips, a legend of Brazil* (London, 1886); and, most important of all, José Basílio da Gama's *The Uruguay. A historical romance of South America* (Berkeley and London, 1982). The translation of *O Uruguai*, Basílio da Gama's epic poem (5 cantos, 1,400 lines), was begun in Santos where the critical preface was also written (signed 'Frank Baker', Burton's usual pseudonym). It was completed at various stages during the 1870s. However, Isabel, a devout Catholic, took offence at what she considered the poem's extreme hostility to the Jesuits and their work among the Indians of South America and prevented publication in Burton's lifetime. It was first published by the University of California Press more than a hundred years later.

Burton also contributed a lengthy introduction to the ENGLISH TRANSLATION (from the original German) of *The captivity of Hans Staden of Hesse ... in 1547–1555 among the wild tribes of Eastern Brazil* (London, 1874).

In July 1868, while on sick leave and waiting for a decision on his next consular appointment, Burton left Santos for first Rio de Janeiro, then Montevideo and from Buenos Aires travelled up the Paraná River to Paraguay to report on the War of the Triple Alliance (the Paraguayan War). He was in Paraguay twice: for three weeks August–September 1868 and two weeks April 1869. In his *Letters from the battlefields of Paraguay* (London, 1870), excellent war reportage which, it is claimed, greatly influenced Conrad in the writing of *Nostromo*, Burton investigates Paraguayan, Argentine and Brazilian sides of the lines and expresses considerable sympathy towards Paraguay's dictator, Francisco Solano López.*

---

*Biographers have been fascinated by Richard Burton, a colourful and sometimes scandalous figure, with attention usually centred on his Middle Eastern travels. Modern biographies include: Fawn Brodie, *The devil drives* (London, 1967); Frank McLynn, *Snow upon the desert* (London, 1990); and Mary S. Lovell, *A rage to live. A biography of Richard and Isabel Burton* (New York, 1999). On Burton in the United States, Brazil and the River Plate, see Frank McLynn, *From the Sierras to the Pampas: Richard Burton's travels in the Americas, 1860–69* (London, 1991). See also Alfredo Cordiviola, *Richard Burton, a traveller in Brazil, 1865–1868* (Lewiston, NY and Lampeter, 2001), a study on Burtons *Explorations of the highlands of Brazil*. For a biography of Lady Burton, see Jean Burton, *Sir Richard Burton's Wife* (London, 1942).

In addition to Richard Burton's *Letters from the battlefields of Paraguay* (see above), there are other contemporary accounts of the Paraguayan War by British authors that include detailed assessments of Brazilian military capabilities and morale, as well as descriptions of land and river battles involving Brazilian troops. These include:

- *The Paraná; with incidents of the Paraguayan War, and South American recollections, from 1861 to 1868* (London, 1868) by **Thomas J. Hutchinson**, the British consul in Rosario (Argentina);

- *The war in Paraguay* (London, 1869) by **George Thompson**, a senior officer of engineers in the Paraguayan army;.

- *Seven eventful years in Paraguay* (London, 1869) by **George Frederick Masterman**, a military apothecary who directed the pharmaceutical service of the Paraguayan forces.

- *La Plata, Brazil, and Paraguay, during the present War* (London, 1869) by **A.J. Kennedy**, a British naval commander patrolling eastern South America, including the Paraná River. The final chapters of Kennedy's book include descriptions of Rio de Janeiro, Petrópolis and Bahia, which he visited on his way back to England.

- **E. Wilson**, *Paraguay: a concise history of its rise and progress; and the causes of the present war with Brazil* (London, 1867) examines the possible economic consequences for Brazil of the outcome of the war. Wilson advocates the cause of Paraguay, arguing that a Paraguayan victory would open up both Paraguay and the interior of Brazil to British commerce and investment.

1870–1914

In 1872 the HMS *Challenger* left Portsmouth on a three-year scientific mission circumnavigating the globe. The expedition was sponsored by the British government and organised by the Royal Society in collaboration with the University of Edinburgh, and aimed at charting the depths, movement and contents of the sea and to collect marine life, minerals and clues to climatic phenomena. The expedition's official findings are found in *The report of the scientific results of the exploring voyage of HMS Challenger during the years 1873–1876* (50 vols, London, Edinburgh and Dublin, 1885–95). Volume one (parts one and two) is a general *Narrative of the voyage*.

Though the *Challenger* spent less than two weeks in Brazil (two days in Fernando de Noronha and eleven days in Bahia during September 1873), the expedition's scientists and ship's officers took advantage of their time there to travel, observe and record aspects of local life and nature:

- **Lord George Campbell**, *Log-letters from the 'Challenger'* (London, 1876, 2nd and 3rd editions 1877) includes short accounts of the visit to Fernando de Noronha, with an interesting description of convicts' fishing methods, and to Bahia, with which Campbell was not particularly impressed.

- **H.N. Moseley**, *Notes by a naturalist on the 'Challenger'* (London, 1879) features by far the fullest and best account of Fernando de Noronha, with descriptions of the convict settlement and the island's flora and fauna. There is also a useful account of Bahia, discussing the general layout of the city, churches, tramways and the German and Swiss hotels at Campo Grande. Mosely spent some of his time outside the city and gives an account of his travels on the British owned and run railway, the villages and sugar plantations that he visited and the flora that he observed.

- **John James Wild**, *At Anchor: a narrative of experiences afloat and ashore during the voyage of H.M.S 'Challenger' from 1872 to 1876* (London, 1878) has only very limited text relating to Brazil, but features some interesting illustrations (Wild was the official artist). There are etchings of convicts on Fernando de Noronha and an excellent large illustration of a cricket match at Campo Grande in Bahia between teams drawn from the Bahia Cricket Club and from the *Challenger*.

- **Sir C. Wyville Thomson**, *Voyage of the 'Challenger', the Atlantic* (2 vols, London, 1877) offers the preliminary scientific results of the mission. Thomson was professor of natural history at the University of Edinburgh and the director of the *Challenger*'s civilian scientific staff. Volume two includes data from Bahia, including temperature readings and details of specimens collected.

- **William James Joseph Spry**, *The cruise of Her Majesty's Ship 'Challenger'* (London, 1876). The engine room lieutenant on board the *Challenger*, Spry included in his book a short general description of the city of Bahia and a brief account of the crew's excursions into the interior of the province.

- **Herbert Swire**, *The voyage of the Challenger, a personal narrative of the historic circumnavigation of the globe in the years 1872–1876* (no place, 1938) is the edited journal of the *Challenger*'s navigating sub-lieutenant. The visit to Fernando de Noronha receives little attention (although there are two sketches of convicts and their small catamarans), but the call at Bahia is described in some detail. There is another account of the cricket march played before British and (somewhat baffled) American and Brazilian spectators.

Henry Alexander Wickham, *Rough notes of a journey through the wilderness from Trinidad to Para, Brazil, by way of the great cataracts of the Orinoco, Atabapo, and the Rio Negro* (London, 1872).

Wickham was an itinerant naturalist whose book mainly describes Central America and Venezuela, with only a few pages concerning his travels in 1870 from the Venezuelan border to Manaus. There is, however, an interesting appendix by James De Vismes Drummond Hay (British consul at Pará) entitled 'Report on the industrial classes in the provinces of Pará and Amazonas, Brazil', commenting on the role of European immigrants, black and Indian Brazilians in the regional economy, especially the rubber industry, and describing the availability of food and accommodation. Although generally poor, the book is significant for the information on rubber it contains. In 1876 Wickham, prompted by the Foreign Office, carried out his legendary 'botanical theft', the unauthorised exportation of 70,000 *hevea brasiliensis* (native rubber) seeds to Kew Gardens and from there to rubber plantations in Asia, which led to the virtual collapse of the Amazon rubber industry. See also Wickham's *On the plantation, cultivation and curing of Para Indian rubber (hevea brasiliensis) with an account of its introduction from the western to eastern tropics* (London, 1908), which includes details of rubber in the wild, the cultivation of the plant and the extraction and cure of rubber latex, along with sketches by Wickham.

Marianne North, *Recollections of a happy life*, ed. Mrs John Addington Symonds (2 vols, London, 1892).

North, a 'botanical globe-trotter' during the 1870s and 1880s and a prolific artist, visited Rio de Janeiro and Minas Gerais in 1872–73. She left a large number of paintings and drawings of both plants and topography, including many of southeast Brazil, to Kew Gardens. There is also an abridged MODERN EDITION, edited by Graham Bateman, which features additional material; see *A vision of Eden. The life and work of Marianne North* (London, Kew, 1980).[14]

PORTUGUESE TRANSLATION: Belo Horizonte, Fundação João Pinheiro, 2001, translated and edited by Ana Lúcia Almeida Gazola and Júlio Jeha.

Michael G. Mulhall, *Rio Grande do Sul and its German colonies* (London, 1873); (with **Edward T. Mulhall**) *Handbook of Brazil* (Buenos Aires, 1877); *The English in South America* (Buenos Aires, 1878); and *Journey to Matto Grosso* [1876] (Buenos Aires, c. 1879).

Edward and Michael Mulhall were the Irish owners and editors of *The Standard*, an English-language newspaper published in Buenos Aires. The book on Rio Grande do Sul is especially valuable, including important accounts on the progress of the province's German inhabitants, information on railways and coal mining and two chapters on the expanding city of Porto Alegre of which there is a very good illustration. The *Handbook* is a guide aimed at investors and others with commercial interests in Brazil.

Marian McMurrough Mulhall, *From Europe to Paraguay and Matto-Grosso* (London, 1877) and *Between the Amazon and the Andes, or Ten years of a Lady's travels in the Pampas, Gran Chaco, Paraguay and Matto Grosso* (London, 1881).

Mulhall was Michael Mulhall's wife and often travelled with him. *From Europe to Paraguay* includes an account of a visit to Rio de Janeiro and Petrópolis, as well as travelling to Mato Grosso with chapters on Corumbá and Cuiabá. Apart from descriptions of the Brazilian Mato Grosso, *Between the Amazon and the Andes* includes a description of Rio Grande do Sul and includes observations concerning German, Irish and Welsh immigrants in that province.

Jacaré Assu, pseud., *Brazilian colonization from an European point of view* (London, 1873).

This is a critical look at prospects in Brazil for European immigrants. The anonymous (British) author examines the experiences of Swiss and

---

14 See also Laura Ponsonby, *Marianne North at Kew Gardens* (Exeter and London, Kew, 1990).

German immigrants in Nova Friburgo (Rio de Janeiro), São Paulo, São Leopoldo (Rio Grande do Sul) and elsewhere to point to the impossibility of 'grafting blackthorn upon banana' — i.e. the immigration of English agricultural labourers, as was being encouraged by colonizing agents in the late 1860s and early 1870s.[15]

R. Stewart Clough, *The Amazons. Diary of a twelve months' journey* (London, 1873).

This book is a record of an 1872 mission of inquiry up the Amazon River made on behalf of the Church of England sponsored, London-based South American Missionary Society. Clough travelled from Belém do Pará to the island of Marajó, and then west to Tabitinga and the Peruvian port of Iquitos, stopping at villages and towns along the way. Although the author is primarily concerned with the spiritual and moral condition of the region's Indian population ('I never realized how low the sons of Adam had fallen'), the diary is particularly interesting for its detailed descriptions of the life of the black slaves whom Clough encountered.

Petros, pseud., *A peep at Brazil* (Buxton, 1876).

This book is a record of a visit to Rio de Janeiro during the early 1870s. The city of Rio de Janeiro is described, but it is the chapters covering the author's travels to Petrópolis and his stay on the coffee producing Fazenda de Monte Lajes, near Macaé, that are especially interesting. There are lengthy accounts of the life of slaves and of carnival.

Charles Barrington Brown and **William Lidstone**, *Fifteen thousand miles on the Amazon and its tributaries* (London, 1878).

Brown (a geologist) and Lidstone (a civil engineer and draughtsman), employees of Amazon Steam Navigation Company, were sent to Brazil to select and report on shipping and port rights allotted to the company. As medical adviser, they were accompanied on their expedition up the Amazon 1873–75 by James William Helenus Trail, a young botanist

---

15 William Scully (see p. 63) was a leading promoter of English and Irish immigration to Brazil. See also Charles Dunlop, *Brazil as a field for emigration* (London, 1866) for a promotional pamphlet by a British author.

and from 1877 professor of botany at the University of Aberdeen.[16] The book features some excellent descriptions of life in the Amazon ports of Obidos, Manaus, Santarém and, especially, Pará, of the Indians in outlying areas and of geological formations.

Thomas Plantagenet Bigg-Wither, *Pioneering in south Brazil. Three years of forest and prairie life in the province of Parana* (2 vols, London, 1878).

Bigg-Wither was a surveyor in Paraná in the early 1870s working on the proposed railway from the Atlantic to the Pacific. There are excellent accounts of surveying work in remote parts of the province, local landowners and their relationship to their workers and the difficulties experienced by English agricultural immigrants. There are also good descriptions of Curitiba and other small towns in Paraná as well as Rio de Janeiro.

PORTUGUESE TRANSLATION: *Novo caminho no Brasil meridional: a provincia do Paraná* (Rio de Janeiro, José Olympio and Curitiba, UFPr, 1974), translation, introduction and notes by Temistocles Linhares.

Also Curitiba, Imprensa Oficial do Paraná, 2001.

J.W. Boddam-Whetham, *Roraima and British Guiana* (London, 1879).

This account of an expedition organised by the colonial government of British Guiana that followed in the footsteps of the Schomburgk brothers (see pp. 55–6) includes observations concerning Indians and other local inhabitants in the British Guiana–Brazil borderlands.

Edward D. Mathews, *Up the Amazon and Madeira rivers through Bolivia and Peru* (London, 1879).

Mathews was an engineer with the Madeira and Mamoré Railway Company. Most of the book concerns the Beni region of Bolivia, but the first four chapters discuss Mathew's voyage in 1874 along the Amazon and its tributaries to the Brazil–Bolivia border. Mathews describes

---

16 *James William Helenus Trail: A memorial volume* (Aberdeen, 1923) provides a biographical sketch and an exhaustive bibliography, including papers published in the *Journal of the Royal Geographical Society* and elsewhere credited to other naturalists drawing on material collected in the Amazon by Trail. See also Magali Romero Sá, 'James William Helenus Trail: a British naturalist in nineteenth century Amazonia', *Historia Naturalis*, vol. 1 (1998).

Belém do Pará, Manaus and other Amazon towns and settlements, the rubber trade, shipping and the life of the people who he meets in his travels.

James W. Wells, *Exploring and travelling three thousand miles through Brazil from Rio de Janeiro to Maranhao* (2 vols, London, 1886).

Wells, a railway engineer, made this journey in 1873–75. His route overlapped in many places with those taken earlier by George Gardner and Richard Burton, whose accounts are rather superior (see pp. 55 and 65). Travelling through the interior of Brazil, heading directly north from Minas Gerais, he described the towns, villages and countryside that he passed through, with accounts of the people he met, the inns or homes where he stayed, local economies and natural history. Wells later wrote an indifferent novel loosely based on his experiences in Brazil: *The Voice of Urbano. A romance of adventures on the Amazons* (1888).

PORTUGUESE TRANSLATION: Belo Horizonte, Fundação João Pinheiro, 1995

Edwin Clark, *A visit to South America* (London, 1878).

In April 1876 Clark, an engineer, travelled from England to Argentina and Paraguay, calling briefly at Pernambuco and Bahia and spending a few days in Rio de Janeiro. Clark's main interest was in meteorology and numerous temperature and other readings are recorded. A general description of Rio de Janeiro is provided, though only the botanical gardens and Tijuca are afforded any detail. Clark also comments on the perils of yellow fever infection in Brazil.

Charles J. Lambert and **(Mrs) S. Lambert**, *The voyage of the 'Wanderer'* (London, 1883).

As part of a world cruise, Mr and Mrs Lambert briefly visited Brazil between October and November 1880. There are short accounts (based on Mr Lambert's journals and Mrs Lambert's letters) of six days spent in Bahia and two weeks in Rio de Janeiro. The Bahia account includes a general description of the city, with some mention of members of the British community there, and of a short railway excursion. For Rio de Janeiro, a journey by rail to Petrópolis is described.

Walter Coote, *Wanderings south and east* (London, 1882).

This is an account of travels in 1881 from Australia to England, by way of the Pacific islands, east Asia and South America. Included is a brief description of the 'quaint city' of Rio de Janeiro, which the author finds much more lively a place than other South American cities that he had visited. Rio's trams are described, as are excursions to Tijuca and Petrópolis. There are also very brief accounts of calls at Bahia and Pernambuco.

Edward Frederick Knight, *The cruise of the 'Falcon': A voyage to South America in a 30-ton yacht* (2 vols, London, 1884).

These volumes record a lone 20-months voyage taken for pleasure in 1880–82 by three English barristers and a cabin boy. Volume one includes a brief description of the city of Bahia and a chapter devoted to Rio de Janeiro (the city, Petrópolis and Paquetá Island). The author particularly expresses an interest in the black inhabitants of these places. Volume two includes a chapter on Pernambuco, but it is the account of the *Falcon*'s visit to the uninhabited islands of Trinidade and Martin Vas that makes the book unusual. Knight describes in some detail the difficulties in landing on the islands, their landscapes and their flora and fauna.

John Ball, *Notes of a naturalist in South America* (London, 1887).

The author spent about a month in Brazil, travelling north from Buenos Aires and arriving in Santos in 1882. He immediately proceeded to São Paulo, but only the briefest of accounts of his stay there is given. Ball provides an account of his railway journey from São Paulo to Rio de Janeiro, commenting on the route taken and providing geological observations. In Rio Ball was much taken by the vegetation of Tijuca and the collections at the botanic gardens. A visit to Petrópolis is described, commenting on the town's villas and regional flora. On his return journey to England, Ball called at Recife, but only the briefest of accounts is given of his short stay there, adding little to this already very slight work.

Ulrick Ralph Burke and **Robert Staples Jr**, *Business and pleasure in Brazil* (London, 1884).

Ulrick Burke was an Irish lawyer and writer, publishing works on Spanish and Mexican history and literature. In 1882 he travelled to

Brazil with a friend, Robert Staples, and though there was no obvious purpose to the trip, a result was this book, a collection of letters, mainly written by Burke, in Brazil. The letters feature observations regarding travel in Brazil. The pair's accommodation and food in Rio de Janeiro — at the Grand Hotel in Botafogo — is described, walks through the city's business district, slaves and slavery, being treated by an American dentist, attending horse races and being received at the royal palace by the emperor. Burke writes of the modernisation of Rio's infrastructure, commenting that it was no surprise that the telephone 'in an enormously straggling town, inhabited by lazy people, is taking wonderfully'. Burke also travels to Petrópolis, which he considers to be more 'civilized' than Rio thanks to its strong German presence, and by rail to Minas Gerais, where he stayed at the Conde d'Eu's *fazenda*. Returning to England from Rio, Burke stopped in Recife, commenting on the theatre there and local society, and very briefly in Maceió.

Hastings Charles Dent, *A year in Brazil, with notes on the abolition of slavery, the finances of the Empire, religion, meteorology, natural history, etc.* (London, 1886).

Dent was a civil engineer on the Minas and Rio Railway. The book gives an account of railway camp life in Minas Gerais but also describes Rio de Janeiro and a visit to Bahia. Dent, a keen botanist and entomologist, records much information on these areas of investigation. Otherwise, his comments are random and generally brief — with regards to mining and railway developments, family life and the local social structure, carnival, slavery and government.

Edward Robert Pearce-Edgcumbe, *Zephyrus; a holiday in Brazil and in the River Plate* (London, 1887).

Over half of this book is devoted to Pearce-Edgcumbe's travels during the mid-1880s in Brazil (Pernambuco, Alagoas, Bahia, Rio de Janeiro and São Paulo), with commentary on the Brazilian landscape and the characters who were encountered. There are separate chapters discussing the persistence of slavery, communications (railways, roads and telephones) and yellow fever. Most pages feature small illustrations detailing a particular aspect of Brazilian life.

Walter Wright, *A few facts about Brazil by a twenty years' resident in that country* (Birmingham and London, 1892).

Wright offers his general impressions of Brazil. There is no obvious periodisation of the author's reminiscences, although the twenty years referred to in the title appears to cover roughly 1870–90. The slave trade, slavery and abolition are discussed and there is a chapter on immigrant labour, including the failure of English immigration. There are also separate chapters on British business, yellow fever and agriculture in Brazil. Brazilian family life was of particular interest to Wright.

May Frances, *Beyond the Argentine; or, letters from Brazil* (London, 1890).

The letters were written in 1887–88, while Frances was visiting her brother, an engineer helping to construct the British-owned Quareim–Itaqui railway line, in western Rio Grande do Sul. Over an 18-month period, Frances writes of the hardships of 'camp' life and of her Brazilian neighbours, the effects of floods, nature and bird life. She regularly visits Uruguaiana (twenty miles away) and other small towns in the region that she describes in some detail. Especially interesting are the author's accounts of British railway employees (both engineers and labourers) and of the lives of the Brazilian women she came to know.

Charles C. Atchison, *A winter cruise in southern seas* (London, 1891).

Instructed by his doctor to escape the English winter and to seek warm weather, Atchison travelled to Brazil and Argentina. The author's diary consists of amusing little vignettes describing life in Pernambuco, Bahia, Rio de Janeiro and Petrópolis. Atchison had only £100 available for his travels and the account includes details of his budget, including shipping and living costs.

Anne Macdonell, *Reminiscences of diplomatic life* (London, 1913).

Lady Macdonell was the Anglo-Argentine wife of Sir Hugh Macdonell, who served as British minister to Brazil from 1885 to 1888. Brazil is the subject of one of the book's chapters. Arriving in Rio de Janeiro in the midst of a major yellow fever outbreak, the couple went immediately to Petrópolis. Diplomatic and court life in both Petrópolis and (in less detail) Rio are described, without a hint of the impending demise of the monarchy.

William Robert Kennedy, *Sporting sketches in South America* (London, 1892).

Kennedy was an admiral with the Royal Navy's South American squadron. His book is an account of off-duty life during three years service in Argentine, Uruguayan, Paraguayan and Brazilian waters in the late 1880s. Although the best sport was found in the River Plate republics, four chapters are devoted to Brazil. Rio de Janeiro, São Paulo, Santos, Bahia and Pernambuco are all described and issues relating to improvements in sports and pastimes, public works and immigration (English and Chinese) are discussed. The islands of Fernando de Noronha and, especially, Trinidade are also described in some detail. Kennedy did much shooting while in Brazil, slaughtering ducks, snipe and partridges at every opportunity.

Ethel Gwendoline Vincent, *China to Peru, over the Andes. A journey through South America* (London, 1894).

In 1893 Mrs Vincent accompanied her husband, the British Member of Parliament Colonel Howard Vincent, on a fact-finding tour of South America to explore political- and trade-related matters. Due to concerns regarding yellow fever, the ship that the Howards were travelling on was unable to call at Recife or other northeastern ports and instead proceeded to Ilha Grande, where the passengers disembarked while the vessel underwent fumigation. Mrs Vincent was struck by the island's beauty, commenting that it was 'very far from being the desolate quarantine station you might suppose'. Although Mrs Vincent visited Botafogo, the botanical gardens and Tijuca, most of the chapter on Rio de Janeiro is devoted to an account of the October 1893 naval rebellion against the dictatorship of Floriano Peixoto, including descriptions of fighting and bombardments that she witnessed. The book's appendices include a newspaper article on the naval rebellion and a report to the Sheffield chamber of commerce on British interests in Brazil, both written by Colonel Vincent.

J.P. Wileman, *Brazilian exchange. The study of an inconvertible currency* (Buenos Aires, 1896).

Wileman was a British civil engineer who lived in Rio Grande in the southern state of Rio Grande do Sul for many years and died in Rio de

Janeriro in 1914. His book was the first systematic analysis of Brazil's financial history, covering the period from 1860 to 1894, and a major influence on the governments of the new Brazilian Republic, and especially Joaquim Murtinho, minister of finance 1898–1902. Other financial histories of the time, for example Liberato de Castro Carreira, *História financeira e orcamentaria do Império* (Rio de Janeiro, 1889; 2nd edition, 1980) were mainly descriptive.

In 1898 Wileman founded the weekly *Brazilian Review* and was its editor until his death in Rio de Janeiro in 1914. He also published *The Brazil yearbook* (2 vols, New York, 1908–09). The *Review* was an important source of economic, financial and business news, aimed at subscribers abroad. After Wileman's death it continued, edited by his son H.F. Wileman, under the title *Wileman's Brazilian Review* until it ceased publication in 1941.

Frederick Alcock, *Trade and travel in South America* (London and Liverpool, 1903).

Included in this book are several chapters directly relating to Brazil, based on a visit that the author made to the region in 1900–01. There is an excellent survey on shipping companies linking Britain with South America, including Brazil, assessments of commercial conditions in different parts of Brazil, and in chapters on Pernambuco and Bahia port facilities are described. The coffee, sugar and rubber trades are discussed and general economic conditions are assessed. The chapter on Rio de Janeiro focuses on the city's usual tourist attractions, though there is also a good description of the island of Paquetá, 'a favourite summer resort for the elite'. The chapter on São Paulo examines the state's railways, the port of Santos and the welfare of recently-arrived immigrants.

Roger Casement, the Irish rebel who was executed in 1916 by the British for high-treason, spent seven years (1906–13) in Brazil as British consul in Santos (in the footsteps of Burton) and Belém do Pará, and then consul-general in Rio de Janeiro. In 1910 Casement, who had already investigated atrocities in the collection of wild rubber in Leopold II's Congo Free State, was directed by the Foreign Office to lead a commission of enquiry being sent to the Putumayo region of the western Amazon (an area straddling the Peruvian–Colombia border) to investigate treatment of the local Indian rubber tappers by the Peruvian Amazon Company. Although Casement did not write a book relating to his Brazilian or Amazonian experiences, journals and diaries credited to him have been published. Especially controversial are the diaries which contain coded, but graphic, accounts of Casement's supposed homosexual encounters in Pará and elsewhere along the Amazon and which were later used as part of a campaign in 1916 to blacken Casement's reputation, but which remained closed to public examination for decades after his execution. See *The Amazon journal of Roger Casement*, edited and with an introduction by **Angus Mitchell** (London and Dublin, 1997), which begins in Belém and Manaus, and R*oger Casement's diaries — 1910: The black and the white* (London, 1997), edited and with an introduction by **Roger Sawyer**.[17]

J.C. Oakenfull, *Brazil in 1909* (Paris, 1910), *Brazil in 1910* (Devonport, 1911), *Brazil in 1911* (Frome and London, 1912), *Brazil in 1913* (Frome, 1913).

These were essentially promotional publications, produced in conjunction with the Brazilian Government Commission of Propaganda and Economic Expansion in Paris. Each edition covered Brazilian history, geography, ethnography, the legal system, literature and the arts, expanding each year with additional topics, especially relating to the agricultural sector of the economy and including photographs. *Brazil: past, present and future* (London, 1919) is an expanded version of the annual it replaced, with the addition of chapters on individual Brazilian regions.

F.A. Coleridge, *Notes on 'the Great River'. The Amazon* (Trichinopoly, South Madras, 1910).

This is a journal by an official on leave from the Indian civil service of a voyage taken from Liverpool along the Amazon to Iquitos and

---

17 Many biographies of Casement have been published, with the following including chapters discussing his consulships in Brazil: B.L. Reid, *The lives of Roger Casement* (New Haven and London, 1976); Roger Sawyer, *Casement: the flawed hero* (London, 1984); Brian Inglis, *Roger Casement* (Belfast, 1993; revised edition London, 2002); Angus Mitchell, *Casement* (London, 2003). See also W.J. McCormack, *Roger Casement in death or haunting the Free State* (Dublin, 2001), which seeks to explain why, despite the weight of evidence, many people have believed that Casement's Amazon diaries were forgeries.

onwards to Porto Velho. Included are observations concerning life in Pará, Manaus and Porto Velho, with a chapter devoted to the development of the Madeira–Mamoré Railway. Especially interesting are descriptions of prisons and police stations in Pará, with the author commenting that, 'police methods of extracting information from witnesses are quite equal to the best Indian Police torture traditions.'

Charles W. Domville-Fife, *The United States of Brazil* (London, 1910).

Domville-Fife was an 'explorer' and journalist, mainly for *The Times*. The book is divided into two parts, the first being a historical survey and the second an examination of contemporary Brazil, with chapters on the Brazilian population, politics and the 'German problem', mining, the Army and Navy and 'Englishmen and English capital in Brazil' as well as short chapters surveying individual states and cities. Domville-Fife later published, besides several books dealing with South America in general, *Among wild tribes of the Amazons. An account of exploration and adventure* (London, 1924), which mainly concerns the population of western Amazonia and the area around Boa Vista, with observations detailing the way of life of different Indian tribes.

James Bryce, *South America. Observations and impressions* (London and New York, 1912).

Bryce was British ambassador in Washington (1907–13) and visited Brazil in 1910 as part of a much wider four-month South American tour. Bryce is extremely timid in his commentary on contemporary Brazil ('[of the political history [...] very little is said in this book, and of their current politics nothing at all. That is a topic on which it would not be fitting for me to enter.'). The most interesting parts of the book are the accounts of travelling through São Paulo and Rio de Janeiro by train and the general comparisons Bryce makes between North and South American history and society.

H.M. Tomlinson, *The sea and the jungle (being the narrative of the voyage of the tramp steamer Capella, 1909 and 1910)* (London, 1912).

Tomlinson, a journalist and novelist, records a journey from England to Pará, along the Amazon and Madeira rivers, and back again. The book, Tomlinson's only enduring literary achievement, is considered a travel literature classic.

Reginald Lloyd (Director), **W. Feldwick, L.T. Delaney, Arnold Wright**, *Twentieth century impressions of Brazil: its history, people, commerce, industries and resources* (London, 1913).

This is a 1000-page, large format directory, illustrated throughout with photographs. It is particularly useful for information (sometimes quite detailed) on individual Brazilian and foreign-owned businesses and for coverage of Brazil beyond Rio de Janeiro.

Joseph Froude Woodoffe, *The upper reaches of the Amazon* (London, 1914).

In 1905 Woodoffe left Liverpool to take up a position with a merchant house in Iquitos, but sometime later the firm ceased trading and he was forced to look elsewhere for work. In the book, the outward journey is described, with accounts of Pará, Santarém, Obidos and, in greater detail, Manaus, a town that Woodoffe returned to later. Much of the account concerns rubber production in both Peruvian (especially around Iquitos and the Putumayo region) and Bolivian Amazon territory. In 1912, Woodoffe took up employment with the Madeira–Mamoré Railway and travelled to Guajará-Mirim (the Brazilian terminus of the line). Apart from an account of life in Guajará-Mirim, there are excellent descriptions of Porto Velho and the surrounding area. The book features a number of good photographs, of which those of the railway are of particular interest. In 1914 Woodoffe returned to England to enlist in the Army, but in the following year *The rubber industry of the Amazon and how its supremacy can be maintained* (London, 1915) was published, featuring contributions from Harald Hamel Smith, the editor of the periodical *Tropical Life*. This book very much focuses on Brazil and, especially, the availability of labour and rubber production methods, though it also discusses food production, hunting and fishing, industry and transport. The life of *seringueiros* is described and suggestions are made as to how to best utilize Amerindian labour. Immigration is a major concern of the book. The author argues that Japanese, Chinese and Siamese men should be imported and encouraged to interbreed with the indigenous population.

Frank Bennett, *Forty years in Brazil* (London, 1914).

Bennett does not explain why — nor even when — he was in Brazil, although he was certainly well travelled and it would appear that he lived in Pernambuco, Rio de Janeiro and Rio Grande do Sul, all of which are described in some detail. Railways in São Paulo are discussed as are marriage habits, holy days and changes in law and society that came about with the advent of the Republic in 1889.

Alured Gray Bell, *The beautiful Rio de Janeiro* (London, 1914).

This richly illustrated (with colour plates and black and white photographs) large format book provides useful text and pictoral images of Rio de Janeiro. After a detailed description of the voyage from Liverpool on a Royal Mail liner, chapters include descriptions of Rio's location, its buildings, shops and businesses, trams, gas and other utilities, public gardens, libraries and the arts, municipal government, local and national politics.

G.J. Bruce, *Brazil and Brazilians* (London, 1915).

Bruce offers a general survey of Brazil on the eve of the First World War with chapters examining the country's history and politics, ethnography, trade and commerce, transportation, entertainment and sport. The background that led to Bruce's interest in Brazil is not explained, nor is it apparent whether he had any first hand experience of the country.

1914–1945

W.H. KOEBEL AND THE SOUTH AMERICAN HANDBOOK

William Henry Koebel, *The Great South Land. The River Plate and southern Brazil of today* (London, 1919).

Koebel was a journalist (writing for the *Times* and the *Standard*, amongst other newspapers) and author of numerous books on New Zealand and, especially, Central and South America, including *South America* (London, 1913) and *British exploits in South America. A history of British activities in exploration, military adventure, diplomacy, science and trade in Latin America* (New York, 1913). *The Great South Land* is the book that contains most on Brazil, contrasting the level of development of the south and southeast of that country with Argentina and Uruguay, countries of which the British public had rather greater knowledge. Koebel explores Brazilian achievements in science and the arts, describes the emergence of Copacabana as a residential district and resort, discusses politics, railway development, cattle raising and agriculture and British and American rivalries in trade and investment in Brazil and compares Rio de Janeiro's British community with that of Buenos Aires.

Koebel's most enduring legacy was *The Anglo-South American Handbook* (London, 1920). After Koebel's death, the guide was purchased by the Royal Mail Steam Packet Co. and reappeared in 1923 as the *South American Handbook*, initially under the joint editorship of **Howell Davies** and **J.A. Hunter** with Davies taking sole charge for four decades (1929–71). The *Handbook* was maintained as an annual publication — even during the Second World War — with the Royal Mail retaining ownership of the title until 1971, by which time the shipping line had abandoned its South American services. Initially aimed primarily at business travellers, the appeal was widened under the editorship of **John Brooks** (1971–89) with the expansion of relatively inexpensive transatlantic air travel during the 1970s. The *South American Handbook* was long considered the best and most detailed guide to the region as a whole. In 1998 the publisher, Footprint, produced the first *Brazil Handbook*, edited by **Ben Box** (who since 1989 had been the editor of *The South American Handbook*), based on an expansion of *The South American Handbook*'s chapter on Brazil. It is now in its third edition.*

---

* *The South American Handbook* and the *Brazil Handbook* are no longer the sole British guide books to Brazil. For example, *The Rough Guide to Brazil* (by David Cleary, Dilwyn Jenkins and Oliver Marshall), first published in 1990 when it was aimed primarily at the needs of budget travellers but subsequently given a much wider appeal, is now entering its fifth edition.

R.B. Cunninghame Graham, *A Brazilian mystic. The life and miracles of Antonio Conselheiro* (London, 1920).

Cunninghame Graham (1852–1936) spent fourteen years of his early adult life in Argentina, Uruguay, Paraguay and the frontier with Brazil. He returned to Scotland in 1883 to become involved in politics, serving as a Liberal member of Parliament, helping with the formation of the Scottish Labour Party and becoming the first president (in 1928) of the Scottish Nationalist Party. Best known for his short stories set in Argentina and Scotland, Cunninghame Graham was the author of *A vanished arcadia* (London, 1901), an extremely romantic account of the expulsion of the Jesuits from South America, as well as *Brazilian mystic* which draws heavily on Euclides da Cunha's classic *Os sertões* (1902).

PORTUGUESE TRANSLATION: São Paulo, Sa Editora/Editora Unesp, 2002.

W. Howarth, *Modern Brazil* (Liverpool, 1923).

Written by an official of the Brazilian consulate-general in Liverpool, this is an up-beat, but dry, survey that explores Brazil's history, government, agricultural and industrial production, finance and banking, customs and trade.

Keith Henderson, *Palm groves and humming birds* (London, 1924).

This rare book (only twenty copies were produced) is a diary of a voyage on a Brazilian naval ship, the *Bagé*, to Brazil by the artist and book illustrator, Keith Henderson. The book is mainly notable for its illustrations, a series of etchings produced by Henderson based on sketches that he made during just two weeks in Recife, Salvador and Rio de Janeiro. The images are of people, buildings, birds, insects and, especially, the luxuriant nature of Rio de Janeiro that impressed him so much.

Archibald Macintyre, *Down the Araguaya; travels in the heart of Brazil* (London, 1925).

In the early 1920s Macintyre travelled through Goiás and Mato Grosso on behalf of the Evangelical Union of South America, a Presbyterian missionary society, to report on the Indian inhabitants of what was still an extremely remote part of Brazil. Different Indian groups — the Kararajá, Javaés, Kayapó and others — are identified and their way of life described. The non-Indian inhabitants are also discussed.

The adventurer **Colonel Percy Harrison Fawcett** had made the eighth and last of his explorations of eastern Bolivia and western Brazil — to Mato Grosso — in 1925. (His first expedition, sponsored by the Royal Geographical Society, had also been to Mato Grosso — in 1906.) *Exploration Fawcett* (London, 1953) was compiled posthumously by **Brian Fawcett**, the author's son, who edited his manuscripts, letters, logbooks and journals and provided an epilogue on his father's disappearance. The hardships of travelling through remote parts of the Brazilian interior are described in detail, as are encounters with Indians and frontier towns such as Corumbá and Cuiabá. Fawcett's disappearance in Mato Grosso in 1925 resulted in enormous public interest in Britain. Several expeditions were sent to Brazil with the aim of finding out what became of the explorer and his party. Numerous books on the search for Fawcett were published: was he killed or kidnapped by Indians or bandits, did he disappear voluntarily or did he somehow simply get lost?[18]

Hugh Pearson, *The diamond trail: an account of travel among the little known Bahian diamond fields of Brazil* (London, 1926).

The author, who had earlier accompanied Peter Younghusband in Tibet, was a member of an early 1920s expedition to investigate the possibility of commercial prospecting for diamonds in the Chapada Diamantina area of northwestern Bahia. Pearson travelled by rail, river and mule to visit isolated mining camps, towns and villages and reported in great detail his impressions of the region. Although diamonds are very much the focus of this book, gold mining is also discussed.

Rudyard Kipling, *Brazilian sketches* (London, 1927; 2nd edition 1928; New York, 1940).

The famous writer records his impressions of Brazil, which he visited

---

18 An American expedition led by George Miller Dyott in 1928 resulted in his *Man hunting in the jungle, being a story of a search for three explorers lost in the Brazilian wilds* (Philadelphia and London, 1930). The book, which features some excellent photographs, concludes that the Fawcett party was most likely killed by Indians. Of later books related to the disappearance of Fawcett, perhaps the most curious is Geraldine Cummins, *The fate of Colonel Fawcett* (London, 1955). Cummings, an Irish mystic and medium with the gift of 'automatic writing', claimed that she received messages from Fawcett in 1935 and 1948-51 in which he stated that he was still in the Mato Grosso living amongst Indians who worshipped him. At Cummins' last sitting in contact with Fawcett, the explorer reported his own death.

early in 1927, aged 62. The accounts of Rio de Janeiro (he was especially taken by Copacabana), Santos and the railway connecting the port with the city of São Paulo and the surrounding coffee estates were clearly very hastily written but provide a useful picture of the pace of change in some of these places.

Kenneth Grubb, *The lowland Indians of Amazonia* (London, 1927) and (with Erasmo Braga) *The republic of Brazil; a survey of the religious situation* (London, 1932).

Grubb enlisted in the Worldwide Evangelization Crusade after the First World War and spent 'four years of lonely exploration of the Upper Amazon' studying over 200 Indian languages. *The lowland Indians of Amazonia* is basically a linguistic survey, but with information also on foreign missionary societies. *The republic of Brazil* is a survey of evangelical Protestant missions in Brazil. Grubb also wrote two useful travel books largely about Brazilian Amazonia: *Amazon and Andes* (1930) and *From Pacific to Atlantic* (1933). At the end of the Second World War Grubb became the first secretary-general of the Hispanic and Luso Brazilian Councils (Canning House), founded in London in 1943.

Terence C. Hanson, *A railway engineer in Brazil* (London, 1989).

Born in India in 1902, Hanson arrived in Brazil in 1927 to work with the Great Western of Brazil Railway. Hanson's first posting was as a district engineer in Maceió and he ended his career in Recife as the railway's chief engineer. Clearly based on diaries, this book provides a detailed account of Hanson's career with the railway and life in Brazil, from his recruitment in London until his retirement from the company in 1959. Engineering problems and solutions in Alagoas, Pernambuco and Natal are discussed, as is the gradual Brazilianisation of the company.

James A. Williamson, *English colonies in Guiana and on the Amazon, 1604–1668* (Oxford, 1933).

This is one of the earliest scholarly works on Brazil by a British historian. Williamson was a master at Westminster City School who wrote many books — both scholarly and popular — on early voyages of exploration and Tudor history. He also edited William Dampier's *A voyage to New Holland ... in the year 1699* (London, 1939) (see p. 16).

Peter Fleming, *Brazilian adventure* (London, 1933).

This was the book about Brazil most read by the British public in the inter-war period. Fleming's first book (he was the literary editor of *The Times* and later wrote on remote regions of China),[19] this is an often humorous account of the British Expedition to Mato Grosso in 1932, an ill-prepared expedition in search of Fawcett. Fleming joined the expedition after answering an advertisement in *The Times* and then travelled out to Rio de Janeiro, from where he proceeded to São Paulo. Following delays in these cities ('a man in a hurry will be miserable in Brazil'), Fleming travelled by train to Riberão Prêto in the interior of the state of São Paulo, a journey and town that is described in some detail. Most of the book concerns Fleming's travels in the wilds of central Brazil, northwards through Goiás and up the Araguaia, Tapirape and Tocantins rivers to Belém, with excellent accounts of the author's encounters with Indians and other inhabitants.

PORTUGUESE TRANSLATION: São Paulo, Marco Zero, 1996.

As a reaction to Fleming's book, **Robert Churchward** (the leader of the British Mato Grosso Expedition) published *Wilderness of fools — An account of the adventures in search of Lieut.-Colonel P.H. Fawcett, D.S.O.* (London, 1936). Churchward claimed that his was 'a more objective account of the country' and sought to provide more information on the supposed scientific basis of the expedition.

Evelyn Waugh, *Ninety-two days* (London, 1934).

This is a book primarily about the novelist and travel writer's visit to British Guiana in 1933 but includes an excellent account of his crossing the frontier to Boa Vista and elsewhere in northern Roraima. Waugh writes amusingly of the region's Brazilian, British, Amerindian, Chinese and German inhabitants, officials of the Border Commission, Catholic missionaries, traders and horse and cattle ranchers.

Roy Sheffield, *Bolivian spy?* (London, 1935).

Sheffield was a professional cricketer (playing with Essex) who left

---

19 For a biography of Fleming, including a chapter on his travels in Brazil, see Duff Hart-Davis, *Peter Fleming* (London, 1974).

England during the winter months. In the early 1930s Sheffield went to Brazil with the intention of travelling down the Paraná River from Mato Grosso to Argentina. On arrival in Brazil he changed his plans (because of border tensions resulting from the Chaco War) and instead travelled by rail and river to a British-owned cattle *fazenda* at Descalvados in Mato Grosso. Life at Descalvados — and the *fazenda*'s British, American and Brazilian workers and the neighbouring Indians — becomes the central theme of the book. The text is accompanied by photographs taken on the *fazenda*.

Thomas Bentley Duncan, *A missionary arrives in Brazil* (London, 1938).

Duncan was a Presbyterian missionary who was sent to Bahia in 1931 by the Evangelical Union of South America. This is a record of six years that Duncan, his wife and children spent in the São Francisco valley before being transferred to São Paulo. Salvador and its Protestant community are visited on the family's outward journey, but most of the book is devoted to describing Duncan's proselytising efforts in Caruarú, Joazeiro and other villages and small towns in the interior of Bahia, his strong views on the need for 'moral regeneration' (not least amongst Catholic priests and their 'housekeepers') and, at some length, the position of women.

Sir Christopher Gibson, *Enchanted trails* (London, 1948).

In 1935 Gibson travelled from Buenos Aires to Paraguay and Brazil to take stock of his family's land holdings. A member of a prominent Scottish-Argentine family with extensive business interests in both Scotland and South America, Gibson — a prolific author — devoted half of this book to describing the life of Brazilian, British and American workers on Estancia Miranda, a cattle ranch in the southwest of the state of Mato Grosso that he was sent to manage.

William J.W. Roome, *The three Freds — martyred pioneers for Christ in Brazil* (London, 1936).

In 1935 three Protestant missionaries (two Australians and one Irish) from the London-based Unevangelized Fields Mission left their field base in Belém to travel down the Upper Xingu River to make contact with groups of Kayapó Indians who were apparently involved in disputes with one another. The missionaries disappeared and this book is by a member of the search party sent to search for the missionaries whom, it was discovered, had been killed. As well as details on the background to the mission's contact with the Kayapó there are photographs of Indians, missionaries, baptisms and religious celebrations.

Horace Banner, *On the trail of the three Freds — Yield Xingu* (London, 1939).

Banner was another missionary with the Unevangelized Fields Mission who took up the cause of 'winning the Kayapó for Christ'. Banner lived among the Gorotire Kayapó from 1937 to 1951 and retained active connections with the Xingu missions for long after. Aimed at supporters back home in Britain, Banner's later books included *The three Freds and after* (London, 1961) and *Long climb on the Xingu* (London, 1963). Although the books are primarily concerned with presenting the work of missionaries in the Xingu region in a favourable light, Banner displays an understanding of the traditions and culture of the Kayapó on which he wrote several scholarly ethnographical articles in the 1970s.

Ernest Hambloch, *His Majesty the President: a study of constitutional Brazil* (London, 1935).

Hambloch first went to Brazil in 1910 (aged 24) to replace Roger Casement (see p. 79), who left immediately on extended leave, as (acting) consul-general in Rio de Janeiro. He spent the next four years there (1910–14), followed after two years in the Balkans by a further twenty years from 1916, first in the consular and diplomatic service (until his resignation in 1927) — he organised the British participation in the 1922 Centennial Exhibition — then as coffee planter, Reuters correspondent in São Paulo, correspondent of the London *Times* in Rio and secretary of the British Chamber of Commerce. *His Majesty the President* is regarded as one of the most perceptive contemporary analyses of the Brazilian political system during the First Republic (1889–1930) and the provisional government of Getulio Vargas (1930–34), beginning with the statement: 'The origin of Brazil's troubles are to be sought in the defects of her political regime'. Hambloch was forced to leave Brazil after the publication of his controversial book, which was seen by nationalists in Brazil, and especially by the Integralistas, as an attack not on presidentialism per se but on President Vargas — by an agent of British capitalism!

PORTUGUESE TRANSLATION: Brasília, Editora Universidade de Brasília, Coleção Temas Brasileiras, vol. 13, 1981.

Also of interest are Hambloch's *British consul: memories of thirty years' service in Europe and Brazil* (London, 1938) and, not least about the reception in Brazil of *His Majesty the President, Here and there: a medley of memories* (London, 1968).

PART III
1945 – c. 2000

Introduction

At the end of the Second World War, despite half a century of decline from the pre-eminent position it had held throughout most of the 19th century, Britain still had significant commercial and financial links with Brazil. Britain remained Brazil's second most important trading partner and source of capital — though now some way behind the United States. And despite Britain's severe post-war economic problems, the opportunity was there possibly to reverse, certainly to slow down, the decline. The Brazilian market was, however, no longer regarded as a high priority, and there was in any case a doubt whether Britain could provide the consumer goods, capital goods and industrial raw materials Brazil now required. As for British investment, the Treasury ruled out any substantial export of capital to Brazil in the immediate post-war period. There was indeed an acceleration of the process of divestment that had begun in the 1930s with, in particular, the selling of British-owned railways and public utilities. Britain's nominal investment in Brazil declined by 50 per cent between 1939 and 1948. Moreover, there was no longer any great interest, official or unofficial, in Brazil, no political will to strengthen Britain's relations with Brazil, On the contrary, they were allowed to decline still further from the 1950s to the 1980s. In the second half of the 20th century Britain largely abandoned its role as a significant actor in the economic and political affairs of Brazil, although there was a modest revival of interest in the 1990s. Its social and cultural influence is also largely a thing of the past.

Nevertheless, somewhat surprisingly, not only did British journalists and travel writers continue to publish interesting books on Brazil during the second half of the 20th century, but British scholars in universities and other research institutions made a major contribution to the academic study of Brazil.

1945–c.1970

CHARLES BOXER AND BRAZIL

British scholarship relating to Brazil in the immediate post-war period was dominated by the historian of the Portuguese empire **Charles R. Boxer** (1904–2000). Boxer came to the study of colonial Brazil via the study of the Dutch and Portuguese languages better to understand the history of Japan. All his early publications while serving in the British Army mostly in the Far East were on east Asia and particularly Japan in the 16th and 17th centuries. After the Second World War (during which he was for four years a Japanese prisoner of war in Hong Kong) he took up in 1947, without any conventional academic credentials, an appointment as Camoens Professor of Portuguese at King's College London (a chair founded in 1917 and held from 1923 to 1936 by Edgar Prestage, a specialist on the diplomatic history of 17th-century Portugal). Boxer made his first visit to Brazil in April 1949 for the IV Congresso Nacional de História held in Rio de Janeiro and published his first (minor) essays on Brazilian colonial history during the following twelve months.

For two months from September to October 1948 Boxer served as a consultant at the Library of Congress in Washington, D.C. and played a principal role in the preparation of the first International Colloquium on Luso-Brazilian Studies which took place in Washington in October 1950 under the auspices of the Library, celebrating its 150th anniversary, and Vanderbilt University, which had recently established an Institute of Brazilian Studies. Boxer took responsibility (with Engel Sluiter, Berkeley) for the panel on Instruments of Scholarship and wrote one of the eight principal papers submitted to that panel: 'Some considerations on Portuguese colonial historiography', later published in the Colloquium's *Proceedings/Atas* (Nashville, 1953). He was the only British scholar to present a paper at the Colloquium.

In the preface to his first monograph dealing in part with colonial Brazil: *Salvador de Sá and the struggle for Brazil and Angola, 1602–1686* (London, 1952; PORTUGUESE TRANSLATION: São Paulo, Companhia Editora Nacional, Coleção Brasiliana, vol. 353, 1973), Boxer wrote, 'English ignorance of Brazilian history can only be described as abysmal.... Hardly a line has been written in this country on the colonial period of Brazilian history since Robert Southey published his three-volume history in 1810–1819'. Following a second visit to Brazil in 1954, Boxer published a second monograph on colonial Brazilian history: *The Dutch in Brazil 1624–1654* (Oxford, 1957; PORTUGUESE TRANSLATION: São Paulo, Companhia Editora Nacional, Coleção Brasiliana, vol. 312, 1961)* and an essay *A great Luso-Brazilian figure: Padre Antônio Vieira SJ 1608–1697* (London, Canning House, 4th annual lecture, 1957). Unfortunately, he postponed (and never returned to) his plan to write a full-scale biography of Vieira. Two further visits to Brazil in 1959 enabled him to complete the research for a third monograph: *The Golden Age of Brazil 1695–1750: growing pains of a colonial society* (Berkeley and Los Angeles, 1962; PORTUGUESE TRANSLATIONS: Rio de Janeiro, Sociedade de Estudos Históricos Dom Pedro II, 1963, preface by Carlos Rizzini; São Paulo, Companhia Editora Nacional, Coleção Brasiliana, 1969; Rio de Janeiro, Editora Nova Fronteira, 2000, preface by Arno Wehling).

A further visit to Brazil in 1963 was less successful and Boxer vowed it would be 'the last for a long time'. In fact he returned only twice — in 1972 for a conference and in 1986 to receive the Dom Pedro II gold medal of the Instituto Histórico e Geográfico Brasileiro. And apart from another essay/lecture, *Some literary sources for the history of Brazil in the 18th century* (Oxford, Taylorian Lecture, 1967), Boxer did not write again specifically on Brazil. However, two general works, *The Dutch seaborne empire*,

---

*Boxer was not the first British historian to write about the Dutch in Brazil. At the end of the 19th century George Edmundson at Brasenose College, Oxford, published a series of three articles on 'The Dutch power in Brazil, 1624–1654', in the *English Historical Review*, vols xi (1896), xiv (1899) and xv (1900).

1600–1800 (London, 1965) and *The Portuguese seaborne empire, 1415–1825* (London, 1969; PORTUGUESE TRANSLATIONS: Lisbon, Edições 70, 1981; São Paulo, Companhia das Letras, 2002), and many of his later publications on Portuguese colonial history (mostly based on lecture series delivered in the United States) — *Race relations in the Portuguese colonial empire 1415–1825* (Oxford, 1963); *Four centuries of Portuguese expansion 1415–1825: a succinct survey* (Johannesburg, 1965); *Portuguese society in the tropics: the municipal councils of Goa, Macau, Bahia, Luanda 1510–1800* (Madison, WI, 1965); *Women and Iberian expansion overseas, 1415–1815* (New York, 1975); *The Church militant and Iberian expansion, 1440–1770* (Baltimore, 1978) — included much of interest on colonial Brazil. Boxer had resigned from the Camoens Chair of Portuguese at King's College in 1967 and, although continuing to base himself in England, accepted a series of posts at universities in the United States, including Yale, where he was professor of the history of the expansion of Europe overseas from 1969 to 1972. He was a great collector of books and manuscripts and in 1965 had agreed to sell his library to the Lilly Library of Indiana University. Half was transferred between 1965 and 1969, the rest only in 1997.**

** There is now an excellent biography of Boxer by the US historian Dauril Alden: *Charles R. Boxer. An uncommon life* (Lisbon: Fundação Oriente, 2001). For a complete list of Boxer's writings, see George West, *A list of the writings of Charles Ralph Boxer published between 1926 and 1984* (London, 1984) and Alden, *Boxer*, Appendix 7, 'The writings of Charles Boxer, 1985–1996.'

Besides Boxer, the only British scholar to attend the first International Colloquium on Luso-Brazilian Studies in Washington in 1950 was **H.V. (Harold) Livermore**. Livermore taught Portuguese at Cambridge immediately after the war before becoming education officer at Canning House (the Hispanic and Luso-Brazilian Councils). He was primarily a scholar of Portuguese literature and history, publishing *A history of Portugal* (Cambridge, 1947) and *A new history of Portugal* (Cambridge, 1966), and from the late 1950s teaching at the University of British Columbia in Vancouver. He did, however, edit (with W.J. Entwistle) the only book published in Britain during the immediate post-war period that attempted, at least in part, to treat modern Brazil, that is to say, Brazil since Independence, in a serious way. *Portugal and Brazil: an introduction* (Oxford, 1953) included eight chapters on Brazil, four of them by British authors: Kenneth Grubb on land and people, R.A. Humphreys, holder — since 1948 — of the Chair of Latin American History at University College London, the only such chair in a British university, on monarchy and empire, Livermore himself on the republic and his wife Ann Livermore on music.

Another British scholar **John Bury**, although unable to attend the Luso-Brazilian Colloquium in Washington, had submitted a paper to the Fine Arts panel ('Portuguese and Brazilian architecture of the 17th and 18th centuries') that was, like Boxer's paper on Portuguese colonial historiography, eventually published in the *Proceedings/Atas* (1953). Bury, however, settled on a business rather than an academic career. Nevertheless, he continued to write and research and made a distinguished contribution to the study of colonial Brazilian art and architecture. The more important of his essays, including a chapter on the art and architecture of colonial Brazil in volume two of the *Cambridge History of Latin America* (1984), were published in *Arquitetura e arte no Brasil colonial* (São Paulo, 1990).

Apart from its colonial history (largely occupied by one man — Boxer) only the Amazon attracted British scholars to Brazil in the post-war period. **Francis Huxley** was the first to do fieldwork among the indigenous peoples of Brazilian Amazonia. His *Affable savages: an anthropologist among the Urubu Indians of Brazil* (London, 1956), a study of the Urubu Indians (now generally known as the Kaapor) in Maranhão and Pará, based on fieldwork in 1951 (alongside the young Brazilian anthropologist Darcy Ribeiro) and in 1953 — for his Oxford DPhil — was a pioneering work. However, after a brief spell at Cambridge, and failing to secure a post in Oxford, Huxley moved out of mainstream academic life.

PORTUGUESE TRANSLATION: *Selvagens amaveis* (São Paulo, Companhia Editora Nacional, Coleção Brasiliana, vol. 316, 1963)

Nicholas Guppy, a Cambridge- and Oxford-educated botanist and specialist on tropical forests (born in Trinidad), spent four years in British Guiana and made several expeditions across the Brazilian border into Roraima to collect plants. *Wai-Wai: through the forests north of the Amazon* (London, 1958) is an account of one of these expeditions, providing insights into the region's Amerindian inhabitants and with many references to previous travellers, such as the Schomburgk brothers (see p. 55).

Although in British universities anthropology remained primarily focused on Africa and Asia, Amazonia became an important field of research at this time, largely as a result of the powerful influence of Claude Levi-Strauss on Rodney Needham in Oxford and Edmund Leach in Cambridge. **David Maybury-Lewis**, a student of Needham, worked in Central Brazil in the late 1950s and wrote the popular *The savage and the innocent* (London, 1965) and the scholarly *Akwe-Shavante society* (Oxford: Clarendon Press, 1967). Maybury-Lewis had moved to Harvard in 1961 immediately after completing his Oxford DPhil — and remained there. His later publications include two edited volumes, *Dialectical societies: the Gê and Bororo of central Brazil* (Cambridge, MA, 1979) and *The attraction of opposites: thought and society in the dualistic mode*) (Ann Arbor, MI, 1989), a collections of essays on Brazilian Indians.

The botanical artist **Margaret Mee** had visited Brazil for the first time in 1952, made the first five of her journeys to the Amazon between 1956 and 1967 and published the most important of her many well-known studies of Brazilian flora *Flowers of the Brazilian forests* in 1968. Her fifteenth and final visit to Brazil was in 1988, the year in which the diaries and sketchbooks of all her journeys were published as *In search of flowers of the Amazon forest* (Woodbridge, Suffolk) edited by Tony Morrison.

Adrian Cowell was a member of the Oxford and Cambridge South American Expedition of 1957–58. After returning to the Xingu area of northern Mato Grosso, he wrote *The heart of the forest* (London, 1960). In the 1970s and 1980s Cowell made the enormously successful and influential television documentaries *The tribe that hides from man* (on the Xingu's Kreen-Akore people) and *A decade of destruction: the crusade to save the Amazon rain forest* (also centred on the Xingu). Both films resulted in books, published in London in 1973 and New York in 1990, respectively.

Sacheverell Sitwell, poet, writer and art historian, who dedicated much of his life to the study of 'Baroque and Rococo and their affiliations in every country where they can be found', wrote *Southern baroque art* (1924) in his early twenties, before he knew either Spain or Portugal. He made his first visit to Latin America (to Mexico) only in 1952, but made a further four visits during the following fifteen years. *Southern baroque revisited* (London, 1967), chapter eight, provides an excellent account of his visit to Rio de Janeiro, Minas Gerais, Bahia and Pernambuco (it is not clear in which year), particularly valuable for his views on Brazilian baroque art and architecture.

An expedition in the late 1960s, organised and led jointly by the Royal Geographical Society and the Royal Society (at the invitation of the Brazilian government), the first British multi-disciplinary venture of its kind, produced besides a mass of research papers (particularly in the new field of *cerrado* studies) an excellent general book by the writer and broadcaster **Anthony Smith**, *Mato Grosso: last virgin land* (London, 1971).

Two young British scholars in the humanities (literature and modern history respectively) who were to play a significant role in the development of Brazilian studies in UK universities from the mid-1960s had visited Brazil for first time in 1960 (indeed they travelled there together — by ship, steerage). **Giovanni Pontiero** (age 28) was researching for a PhD in Brazilian literature at Glasgow University (under the supervision of Professor William C. Atkinson, head of the Department of Hispanic Studies and author of the Penguin *History of Spain and Portugal*, 1960). **Leslie Bethell** (age 23) was researching for a PhD in Latin American history at University College London (under the supervision of Professor R.A. Humphreys, who held the only Chair of Latin American History in the country at the time). A pamphlet written by Atkinson for the British Council in the early 1970s, *British contributions to Portuguese and Brazilian studies* (1974) — a revised and updated version of a pamphlet originally published in 1945 — is mainly concerned with Portugal. On Brazil it finds worthy of note in the entire thirty years since the end of the Second World War only Boxer's monographs, the volume of essays edited by Livermore and Entwistle, and the first books by Pontiero (*Anthology of Brazilian modernist* *poetry*, 1969) and Bethell (*Abolition of the Brazilian slave trade*, 1970), although in fact, as we shall see, by the time Atkinson published his pamphlet the following books from the new generation of British academic 'Brazilianists' had also been published: A.J.R. Russell-Wood, *Fidalgos and philanthropists* (1968), Emanuel de Kadt, *Catholic radicals in Brazil* (1970), Peter Rivière, *The forgotten frontier* (1972) and Kenneth Maxwell, *Conflict and conspiracies* (1973) (see below).

c. 1970 – c. 2000

The Parry report (1965)

In October 1962 the University Grants Committee set up a sub-committee under the chairmanship of Professor J.H. Parry (and including among its members both Charles Boxer and R.A. Humphreys) 'to review development in the universities in the field of Latin American Studies and to consider and advise on proposals for future developments'. It presented its report in August 1964. The opening sentences of Chapter 1 'Summary of Findings and Recommendations' reads: 'The state of Latin American studies in British universities entirely fails to reflect the economic, political and cultural importance of Latin America. It reflects, instead, a lack of interest in, and a general ignorance about, this great area in Great Britain'. Only isolated individuals studied Latin America and none of the leading figures studied Brazil, with the singular exception of Charles Boxer himself — and he always made a point of saying that he knew nothing of Brazil after its separation from Portugal in 1822.

The *Report on the future of Latin American studies in the UK* (the Parry Report) (published in 1965) led to the creation of institutes or centres of Latin American studies during the second half of the decade in five universities: London, Cambridge, Glasgow, Liverpool and Oxford. The University of Essex (founded in 1965) did not receive Parry funding but it nevertheless established a centre for Latin American studies, which was generally regarded as a sixth Parry centre. Named posts (lectureships in Latin American politics, economics, sociology, etc.), studentships, research and travel funds were made available and eventually transformed teaching and research and publication on Latin America in the United Kingdom. Brazil, however, was relatively neglected in these institutes and centres, with the exception of Liverpool in its early days where John Dickenson (geography), John Gledson (literature), Giovanni Pontiero (literature) and Peter Flynn (politics) all worked and later published books on Brazil, Glasgow under the directorship of Peter Flynn (1972–97) and London under the directorship of Leslie Bethell (1987–92). In 1997 Oxford University established a Centre for Brazilian Studies separate from its Latin American Centre and appointed Leslie Bethell its first director.

Outside the designated 'Parry' institutes and centres of Latin American studies — in the various colleges of the universities of London, for example, and in universities without such institutes/centres — individual scholars in departments of history, geography, anthropology, etc., and not least in departments of modern languages, romance languages, Spanish and Portuguese and Latin American studies, continued to study Brazil.

And there was important research activity on Brazil outside the universities, most notably at the Royal Botanic Gardens, Kew (where Ghillean Prance became director in 1989), the Royal Botanic Garden, Edinburgh, and the Royal Geographical Society (where John Hemming was director and secretary, 1975–96).

There was, therefore, after c. 1970, a significant increase in the number of scholarly publications on Brazil — journal articles, research papers, chapters in books as well as the books that are the subject of this survey — by 'Brazilianists' in British universities and other research institutions. Among the leading 'pioneers' in the 1970s and 1980s were:

Giovanni Pontiero

After first visiting Brazil in 1960 Pontiero taught at the University of Liverpool in the late 1960s and published his first book *An anthology of Brazilian modernist poetry* (Oxford, 1969), see above. He then taught at the University of Manchester from 1970 until his untimely death in 1992. He published three more books on Brazilian poetry: *Carlos

Nejar: poeta e pensador (Porto Alegre, 1984); *Os Personae — poemas de Carlos Nejar* (Porto Alegre, 1986); and *Manuel Bandeira (visão geral de sua obra)* (Rio de Janeiro, 1986).

Pontiero was also a distinguished, prize-winning translator of the Portuguese novelist Jose Saramago and of several Brazilian poets and novelists. Perhaps his greatest contribution to Brazilian literature was the translation into English of many of the novels and short stories of Clarice Lispector (with critical introductions): *Family ties: stories and chronicles* [*Laços de familia*] (Austin, Texas, 1972; 2nd revised edition, 1984); *The foreign legion* [*A legião estrangeira*] (Manchester 1986); *The hour of the star* [*A hora da estrela*] (Manchester, 1986); *Near the wild heart* [*Perto do coração selvagem*] (Manchester, 1990); *Discovering the world* [*A descoberta do mundo*] (Manchester, 1992); and *The besieged city* [*A cidade sitiada*] (Manchester, 1997). His other translations of Brazilian writers included Ana Miranda, *The Bay of All Saints and every conceivable sin* (*Boca do inferno*) (London, 1991).

Leslie Bethell

After going to Brazil for the first time in 1960, Bethell taught European history at Bristol University until his appointment in 1966 to the first post established in a British university specifically to include Brazil in its title: a Lectureship in Hispanic American and Brazilian History at University College London. He held the lectureship (later readership) until his appointment to the University of London Chair of Latin American History (formerly held by R.A Humphreys and John Lynch) in 1986, which from 1987 was combined with the directorship of the University of London Institute of Latin American Studies. In 1993, after a year at the University of Chicago, Bethell was appointed to a Baring Foundation Senior Research Fellowship in Brazilian Studies at St Antony's College Oxford, and in 1997 to the directorship of the newly established University of Oxford Centre for Brazilian Studies.

Bethell's first book was *The abolition of the Brazilian slave trade. Britain, Brazil and the slave trade question, 1807–1869* (Cambridge, 1970). In the late 1970s he began editing the *Cambridge History of Latin America (CHLA)*. The first five volumes were published in 1984–86: Vol. I *Colonial Latin America* (1984); Vol. II *Colonial Latin America*

(1984); Vol. III *Latin America from Independence to c.1870* (1985); Vol. IV *Latin America: c. 1870 to 1930* (1986); Vol. V *Latin America: c. 1870 to 1930* (1986). The chapters on Brazil were also published separately: Leslie Bethell, ed., *Colonial Brazil* (Cambridge, 1987) and *Brazil: Empire and Republic (1808–1930)* (Cambridge, 1989). CHLA Vol. VI *Latin America since 1930: economy, society and politics*. Part 1 Economy and society, Part 2 Politics and society (1994) and Vol. X *Latin America since 1930: ideas, culture and society* (1995) contain a good deal on Brazil. CHLA vol. IX on Brazil since 1930 remains to be completed. The *Cambridge History* is being published in PORTUGUESE TRANSLATION by Editora da Universidade de São Paulo (Edusp). Bethell's later publications include an edited volume *Brasil: fardo do passado, promessa do futuro. Dez ensaios sobre política e sociedade brasileira* (Rio de Janeiro, 2002).

Emanuel de Kadt

De Kadt was a Dutch-born sociologist who, after almost a decade at the London School of Economics, moved to the Institute of Development Studies at the University of Sussex in 1969, where Brazil became only one of his concerns. *Catholic radicals in Brazil* (Oxford, 1970), based on fieldwork in Brazil in the 1960s for his London PhD, focuses on the Movimento de Educação de Base (MEB), a Church sponsored, government financed movement active in the rural areas immediately before and after the military coup of 1964.

Peter Rivière

Rivière, like David Maybury-Lewis (see p. 100) a student of Rodney Needham at Oxford, went to Brazil for the first time in 1957 with the Oxford and Cambridge South American Expedition. He returned to Oxford and remained at the Institute of Social and Cultural Anthropology (and Linacre College) for the rest of his academic career, until retirement in 2001, mainly researching on the Indians of Guiana but writing on Brazil (both anthropology and history). *The forgotten frontier: ranchers of northern Brazil* (New York, 1972) was followed by *Individual and society in Guiana: a comparative study of Amerindian social organisation* (Cambridge, 1984; PORTUGUESE TRANSLATION: São Paulo, Edusp, 2001), an ethnographic study of lowland northeast South America that includes the native peoples of Brazil (Aparí, Trio, Waiyana, Waiwai, Macusi and Wapishiana) to the immediate south of Guyana, Suriname and French Guiana. *Absent minded imperialism: Britain and the expansion of empire in nineteenth century Brazil* (London, 1995) is a study of the drawing of the border between Brazil and British Guiana.

John Hemming

Hemming, an Oxford history graduate, was a member of the ill-fated 1961 expedition to the Amazon in which Richard Mason lost his life at the hands of the Kreen-Akrore Indians (now called the Panara). He went into the family business but continued to research and write on Brazil, becoming Britain's leading specialist on the Amazon and particularly on the history of Brazil's indigenous peoples. He retired from the directorship of the Royal Geographical Society in 1996 after more than twenty years. *Red gold: the conquest of the Brazilian Indians 1500–1760* (London, 1978), *Amazon frontier: the defeat of the Brazilian Indians* (London, 1987), the history of Brazil's indigenous people in the late 18th and 19th centuries, and *Die if you must: Brazilian Indians in the twentieth century* (London, 2003) together constitute a major contribution to the history of Brazil's Indians. Hemming also edited an important two-volume collection of papers on contemporary Amazonia: *Change in the Amazon Basin*. Vol. 1 *Man's impact on forests and rivers*, Vol. 2 *The frontier after a decade of colonisation* (Manchester, 1985).

In 1987–88 Hemming led the Maracá Rainforest Project (Projeto Maracá), organised by the Royal Geographical Society in London at the invitation of the Brazilian Secretária Especial do Meio Ambiente (SEMA — now part of Instituto Brasilero do Meio Ambiente e dos Recursos Naturais Renováveis, or IBAMA), in partnership with Instituto Nacional de Pesquisas da Amazônia (INPA) in Manaus, which set out to record and document the ecological structure of a relatively undisturbed section of the Brazilian rainforest. With more than 200 scientists and technicians, it was the largest research effort ever mounted by a European country in Amazonia and produced a number of important publications by Hemming himself and two botanists at the Royal Botanic Garden, Edinburgh: James A. Ratter, one of the world's leading authorities on the *cerrado*, and William Milliken, botanist and ethnologist (see p. 118).

Peter Flynn

Flynn, who became Britain's leading specialist on Brazilian politics, had gone to Brazil for the first time in 1965 as a graduate student at St Antony's College, Oxford. After some years at the University of Liverpool, he replaced W.C. Atkinson as director of the Institute of Latin American Studies at the University of Glasgow in 1972 and retained the post until the closure of the Institute in 1997. *Brazil: a political analysis* (London, 1978) is a political history of Brazil from the revolution of 1930 to the mid point in the 21-year military regime that followed the *golpe* of 1964 (the presidency of Ernesto Geisel beginning in 1974). Besides innumerable articles on Brazilian political history and Brazilian politics Flynn was also the co-editor (with H. Jaenecke) of *Sustainable land use systems and human living conditions in the Amazon* (Brussels, 1992).

John P. Dickenson

Dickenson, a geographer with an interest in British naturalists in 19th-century Brazil, taught in the Institute of Latin American Studies at Liverpool University from the late 1960s until his early retirement in the 1990s. He is the author of two studies on Brazilian geography: *Studies in industrial geography: Brazil* (Folkestone, 1978) and *Brazil* (London, 1982), as well as an important contribution to Brazilian bibliography: Brazil World bibliographical series, vol. 57 (revised edition) (Oxford and Santa Barbara, 1997).

Anthony Hall

Hall, who first visited Brazil in 1969 and has a PhD from the University of Glasgow, has been at the London School of Economics since 1983. He is the UK's leading specialist on the economic, social and environmental problems of the Brazilian northeast and Amazonia. His books include *Drought and irrigation in north-east Brazil* (Cambridge, 1978); *Developing Amazonia: deforestation and social conflict in Brazil's Carajas programme* (Manchester, 1989); *Sustaining Amazonia: grass-roots actions for productive conservation* (Manchester, 1997); (edited with David Goodman) *The future of Amazonia: destruction or sustainable development?* (London, 1990); and, another edited volume, *Amazonia at the crossroads: the challenge of sustainable development* (London, 2000).

John Gledson

Gledson, the leading British specialist on Brazilian literature and culture, first visited Brazil in 1970 as a PhD student at Princeton. He then taught at the University of Liverpool from 1973 until his early retirement in 1994. He is the author of *Poesia e poetica de Carlos Drummond de Andrade* (São Paulo, 1981) and two important studies on Machado de Assis: *The deceptive realism of Machado de Assis: a dissenting interpretation of Dom Casmurro* (Liverpool, 1984) and *Machado de Assis: ficção e historia* (Rio de Janeiro, 1986). He has edited two volumes of Machado's *cronicas*: *Bons dias!* (São Paulo, 1989) and *A semana 1892–1932* (São Paulo, 1996) as well as *Contos. Uma antologia* (São Paulo, 1999). Gledson is also an internationally recognised translator of Brazilian literature, especially the novels of Machado de Assis, with a critical edition of *Dom Casmurro* (New York, 1997), and of one of Brazil's leading literary essayists, Roberto Schwarz: *Misplaced ideas: essays on Brazilian culture* (London, 1992) and *A master on the periphery of capitalism: Machado de Assis* (Durham, NC, 2001). See also Milton Hatoum, *The brothers* (*Dois irmãos*) (London, 2002).

Joe Foweraker

Joe Foweraker has spent most of his career at Essex University, where he is now professor of sociology. He is the author of *The struggle for land: a political economy of the pioneer frontier in Brazil from 1930 to the present day* (Cambridge, 1981), a ground-breaking study of the land question in Brazil and (with Tod Landman) *Citizenship rights and social movements: a comparative and statistical analysis* (London, 1997), on Spain, Mexico, Chile and Brazil.

John Humphrey

John Humphrey, a leading sociologist at the Institute of Development Studies, Sussex University, is the author of two important studies on Brazil published in the 1980s: *Capitalist control and workers' struggle in the Brazilian auto industry* (Princeton, 1982) and *Gender and work in the Third World: sexual divisions in Brazilian industry* (London, 1987).

David Brookshaw

David Brookshaw has taught Brazilian literature at the University of Bristol since 1978, after a spell at Queen's University, Belfast. He is the author of *Raça e cor na literatura brasileira* (Porto Alegre, 1983; ENGLISH TRANSLATION: *Race and colour in Brazilian literature*, London, 1986) and *Paradise betrayed: Brazilian literature of the Indian* (Amsterdam, 1989).

David Treece

A student of John Gledson at Liverpool, Treece became lecturer in the Department of Portuguese and Brazilian Studies at King's College London in 1987 and reader and director of the department's newly established Centre for the Study of Brazilian Society and Culture, which concentrates on research into Brazilian popular culture, in 1996. He is the author of *Exiles, allies, rebels: Brazil's Indianist movement, indigenist politics and the imperial nation-state* (London, 2000). Treece is also a highly respected translator of Brazilian literature into English. See, for example, Caio Fernando Abreu, *Dragons* (*Os dragões não conhecem o paraíso*) (London, 1990); João Gilberto Noll, *Hotel Atlântico* (from *Hotel Atlântico* and *Harmada*) (London, 1997); (edited with Patricia E. Paige and Celia McCullough) Ana Cristina Cesar, *Intimate diary* (London, 1997); and João Guimarães Rosa, *The jaguar and other stories* (Oxford, 2001).

Some British 'Brazilianists' pursued their academic careers outside Britain. For example,

- **A.J.R. Russell-Wood**, who after completing his DPhil at Oxford University and publishing *Fidalgos and philanthropists: the Santa Casa de Misericordia of Bahia, 1550–1775* (Berkeley and Los Angeles, 1968) moved to the Johns Hopkins University in 1971 and has remained there. His many other important publications in the field of Brazilian colonial history include *The black man in slavery and freedom in colonial Brazil*

(London, 1982); *Society and government in colonial Brazil, 1500–1822.* (Aldershot, 1992); *A world on the move: the Portuguese in Africa, Asia and America, 1415–1808* (Manchester, 1992) — new edition appearing as *The Portuguese empire, 1415–1808: a world on the move* (Baltimore, 1998).

- **Kenneth R. Maxwell**, who after taking his first degree at Cambridge University, began research for his PhD at Princeton under the supervision of Stanley Stein (published as *Conflicts and conspiracies: Brazil and Portugal, 1750–1808*, Cambridge, 1973). He remained in the United States and made his career in New York (at the Tinker Foundation, Columbia University and the Council on Foreign Relations), more a specialist on Portugal than Brazil. His later publications include *Pombal. Paradox of the Enlightenment* (Cambridge, 1995) and *Naked tropics. Essays on empire and other rogues* (New York, 2003).

- **Nancy Leys Stepan**, who after completing her PhD at UCLA in 1971 also remained in the United States (mainly at Columbia University). Her publications include *Beginnings of Brazilian science: Oswaldo Cruz, medical research and policy,1890–1920* (New York, 1976), *'The hour of eugenics': race, gender and nation in Latin America* (Ithaca, NY, 1991), a study of the social and scientific movement for 'modernisation' and race improvement, which had a major influence on doctors, lawyers and public hygiene experts in Brazil and elsewhere during the inter-war years, and *Picturing tropical nature* (London, 2001), a reflection on attitudes of 19th and 20th century European and North American travellers, artists and scientists to tropical nature and landscape, people and disease, with particular reference to Brazil.

- **Nigel J.H. Smith**, a bio-geographer, who made his career at the University of Florida, Gainesville. His many books include: *Rainforest corridors: the Transamazon colonisation scheme* (Berkeley and London, 1982), *The Amazon River Forest: a natural history of plants, animals and people* (New York and Oxford, 1999) and *Amazon sweet sea. Land, life and water at the river's mouth* (Austin, TX, 2002).

- **Roderick J. Barman**, who after taking his PhD at the University of California, Berkeley, in 1970 settled in Canada and teaches at the University of British Columbia in Vancouver. He is the author of *Brazil. The forging of a nation, 1798–1852* (Stanford, 1988), *Citizen Emperor. Pedro II and the making of Brazil, 1825–1891* (Stanford, 1999) and *Princess Isabel of Brazil, gender and power in the nineteenth century* (Wilmington, DE, 2002).

- **Peter Fry**, a social anthropologist, who went to Brazil in 1970 after completing a PhD at University College London and remained there — first at the Universidade Estadual de Campinas (UNICAMP), then at the Universidade Federal do Rio de Janeiro (UFRJ). His books include: *Para inglês ver: identidade e política na cultura brasileira* (São Paulo, 1982) and (with Carlos Vogt) *Cafundó. A África no Brasil: linguagem e sociedade* (Campinas, SP, 1996).

- **Ghillean Prance**, a distinguished botanist, who was the first director of postgraduate studies at INPA in Manaus in the mid-1970s and curator of Amazonian botany and co-ordinator of the Projeto Flora Amazonica at the New York Botanical Garden, 1977–87 before moving to the Royal Botanic Gardens, Kew as director in 1989. His many books on Brazil include: (with M.F. da Silva) *Arvores de Manaus* (Belém, 1976), *Amazonia* (London, 1985) (edited with Thomas Lovejoy), *Tropical forests and world climate* (London, 1986) and *Manual da botânica econômica do Maranhão* (São Luis, 1988).

In the 1990s important monographs on Brazil were also published by the following scholars in British universities:

- **Dawn Ades** (art history, University of Essex), **Alan Tormaid Campbell** (social anthropology, University of Edinburgh), **David Cleary** (social anthropology, Universities of Glasgow, Edinburgh and Cambridge before moving to Harvard and then to Brazil), **Michael Eden** (geography, Royal Holloway College,

University of London), **David Lehmann** (social anthropology/development studies, University of Cambridge), **Stephen Nugent** (anthropology, Goldsmiths' College, University of London), **Vivian Schelling** (literature/cultural studies, University of East London), **Joseph Smith** (history/international relations, University of Exeter)

and representative of a new generation of British 'Brazilianists':

- **Edmund Amann** (economics, Centre for Brazilian Studies, Oxford, and subsequently the University of Manchester), **Mark Dineen** (literature/cultural studies, University of Southampton), **Mark Harris** (anthropology, St Andrews University), **Lisa Shaw** (cultural studies, University of Leeds) and **Claire Williams** (literature, University of Liverpool).

A checklist of academic books on Brazil by British scholars, c. 1970–c. 2000 (by discipline):

HISTORY:

Colonial History

- **A.J.R. Russell-Wood**, *Fidalgos and philanthropists: The Santa Casa de Misericordia of Bahia, 1550–1775* (Berkeley and Los Angeles, 1968).

    PORTUGUESE TRANSLATION: Brasília, Editora da Universidade de Brasília, 1981.

- **Kenneth R. Maxwell** *Conflicts and conspiracies: Brazil and Portugal, 1750–1808* (Cambridge, 1973).

    PORTUGUESE TRANSLATION: São Paulo, Editora Paz e Terra, 1977.

- **John Hemming**, *Red gold: the conquest of the Brazilian Indians 1500–1760* (London, 1978).

- **A.J.R. Russell-Wood**, *The black man in slavery and freedom in colonial Brazil* (London, 1982).

- **Leslie Bethell**, ed., *Colonial Brazil* (Cambridge, 1987).

- **Joyce Lorimer**, *English and Irish settlement on the River Amazon, 1550–1646* (London, Hakluyt Society, 1989).

- **P.J.P. Whitehead** and **M. Boeseman**, *A portrait of Dutch 17th century Brazil: animals, plants and people by the artists of Johan Maurits of Nassau* (Amsterdam, 1989).

- **A.J.R. Russell-Wood**, *Society and government in colonial Brazil, 1500–1822* (Aldershot, 1992).

- **Kenneth R. Maxwell**, *Naked tropics. Essays on empire and other rogues* (New York, 2003).

19th and 20th Century History

- **Leslie Bethell**, *The abolition of the Brazilian slave trade: Britain, Brazil and the slave trade question, 1807–1869* (Cambridge, 1970).

    PORTUGUESE TRANSLATIONS: Rio de Janeiro and São Paulo, Expressão e Cultura/Edusp, 1976; Brasília, Editora do Senado Federal, 2002.

- **Nancy Leys Stepan**, *Beginnings of Brazilian science: Oswaldo Cruz, medical research and policy, 1890–1920* (New York, 1976).

    PORTUGUESE TRANSLATION: Rio de Janeiro, Editora Artenova, 1976.

- **John Hemming**, *Amazon frontier: the defeat of the Brazilian Indians* (London, 1987).

- **Roderick J. Barman**, *Brazil. The forging of a nation, 1798–1852* (Stanford, 1988).

- **Leslie Bethell**, ed., *Brazil Empire and Republic, 1808–1930* (Cambridge, 1989).

- **Joseph Smith**, *Unequal giants: diplomatic relations between the United States and Brazil, 1889–1930* (Pittsburgh, 1991).

- **Peter Rivière**, *Absent minded imperialism. Britain and the expansion of empire in nineteenth-century Brazil* (London, 1995).

- **Roderick J. Barman**, *Citizen Emperor. Pedro II and the making of Brazil, 1825–1891* (Stanford, 1999).

- **David Treece**, *Exiles, allies, rebels: Brazil's Indianist movement, Indigenist politics and the Imperial nation-state* (London, 2000).

- **Roderick J. Barman**, *Princess Isabel of Brazil, gender and power in the nineteenth century* (Wilmington, DE, 2002).

- **Joseph Smith**, *A history of Brazil 1500–2000* (London, 2002).

- **John Hemming**, *Die if you must. Brazilian Indians in the twentieth century* (London, 2003).

CULTURAL STUDIES:

Literature

- **Giovanni Pontiero**, *An anthology of Brazilian modernist poetry* (Oxford, 1969).

- **John Gledson**, *Poesia e poetica de Carlos Drummond de Andrade* (São Paulo, 1981).

- **Laurence Hallewell**, *Books in Brazil: a history of the publishing trade* (Metuchen, NJ and London, 1982).

  PORTUGUESE TRANSLATION: *O livro no Brasil (sua historia)*, São Paulo, T.A. Quieroz/Edusp, 1985.

- **David Brookshaw**, *Raça e cor na literatura brasileira* (Porto Alegre, 1983).

  ENGLISH TRANSLATION: *Race and colour in Brazilian literature* (London, 1986).

- **John Gledson**, *The deceptive realism of Machado de Assis: a dissenting interpretation of Dom Casmurro* (Liverpool, 1984).

  PORTUGUESE TRANSLATION: São Paulo, Companhia das Letras, 1991.

c. 1970 – c. 2000

- **Giovanni Pontiero**, *Carlos Nejar: poeta e pensador* (Porto Alegre 1984).
- **Giovanni Pontiero**, *Os Personae — poemas de Carlos Nejar* (Porto Alegre, 1986).
- **Giovanni Pontiero**, *Manuel Bandeira (visão geral de sua obra)* (Rio de Janeiro 1986).
- **John Gledson**, *Machado de Assis: ficção e história* (Rio de Janeiro, 1986).
- **David Brookshaw**, *Paradise betrayed: Brazilian literature of the Indian* (Amsterdam, 1989).
- **Mark Dineen**, *Listening and the people's voice. Erudite and popular literature in northeast Brazil* (London, 1996).
- **Bernard McGuirk** (with **Solange Ribeiro de Oliveira**), ed., *Brazil and the discovery of America: narrative, history, fiction, 1492–1992* (Lewiston, NY and Lampeter, 1996).
- **Claudia Pazos-Alonso** and **Claire Williams**, eds, *Closer to the wild heart: essays on Clarice Lispector* (Oxford, European Humanities Research Centre, 2002).

Music

- **Simon Wright**, *Villa-Lobos* (Oxford, 1992).
- **Lisa Shaw**, *The social history of the Brazilian samba* (Aldershot, 1999).

Art

- **Dawn Ades**, *Siron Franco* (Rio de Janeiro, 1995).
- **Mark Dineen**, ed., *Brazilian woodcutprints* (London, 2001).

SOCIAL SCIENCES:

- **Maria D'Alva Kinzo** and **Victor Bulmer-Thomas**, eds, *Growth and development in Brazil. Cardoso's real challenge* (London, Institute of Latin American Studies, 1995)

- **Leslie Bethell**, ed., *Brasil: fardo do passado, promessa do futuro. Dez ensaios sobre política e sociedade brasileira* (Rio de Janeiro, 2002).

  Essays originally published in English in *Daedalus*, the Journal of the American Academy of Arts and Sciences, Vol. 129/2 (Spring 2000).

- **Maria D'Alva Kinzo** and **James Dunkerley**, eds, *Brazil since 1985: economy, polity and society* (London, Institute of Latin American Studies, 2003).

Government and Politics

- **Emanuel de Kadt**, *Catholic radicals in Brazil* (Oxford, 1970).

- **Peter Flynn,** *Brazil: a political analysis* (London, 1978).

- **Lourdes Sola**, **Eduardo Kugelmas** and **Laurence Whitehead**, eds, *Banco Central. Autoridade política e democratização — um equilíbrio delicado* (São Paulo, 2002).

Economics

- **Edmund Amann**, *Economic liberalisation and industrial performance in Brazil* (Oxford, 2000).

- **Edmund Amann** and **Ha-Joon Chang**, eds, *Brazil and South Korea: economic crisis and restructuring* (London, Institute of Latin American Studies, 2003).

Geography

- **Janet D. Henshall** and **R.P. Momsen**, *A geography of Brazilian development* (London, 1974).

- **J.P. Dickenson**, *Studies in industrial geography: Brazil* (Folkestone, 1978).

- **J.P. Dickenson**, *Brazil* (London, 1982).

Sociology/Social Anthropology

- **Peter Rivière**, *The forgotten frontier: ranchers of northern Brazil* (New York, 1972).

- **Anthony Hall**, *Drought and irrigation in north-east Brazil* (Cambridge, 1978).

- **Joe Foweraker**, *The struggle for land: a political economy of the pioneer frontier in Brazil from 1930 to the present day* (Cambridge, 1981).
  PORTUGUESE TRANSLATION: Rio de Janeiro, Zahar, 1982.

- **Simon Mitchell**, ed., *The logic of poverty: the case of the Brazilian northeast* (London, 1981).

- **Peter Fry**, *Para inglês ver: identidade e politica na cultura brasileira* (São Paulo, 1982).

- **John Humphrey**, *Capitalist control and workers' struggle in the Brazilian auto industry* (Princeton, 1982).
  PORTUGUESE TRANSLATION: *Fazendo 'o milagre'*, Petrópolis, Vozes, 1982.

- **John Humphrey**, *Gender and work in the Third World: sexual divisions in Brazilian industry* (London, 1987).

- **Peter Fry** (with **Carlos Vogt**), *Cafundó. A África no Brasil: linguagem e sociedade* (Campinas, 1996).

- **David Lehmann**, *Struggle for the spirit: Religious transformation and popular culture in Brazil and Latin America* (Oxford, 1996).

AMAZONIAN STUDIES:

Sociology/Social Anthropology/Anthropology/Ethnography/Archaeology

- **Peter Rivière**, *The forgotten frontier: ranchers of northern Brazil* (New York, 1972).

- **Elizabeth Carmichael**, ed., *The hidden peoples of the Amazon* (London, British Museum, 1985).

- **Alan Tormaid Campbell**, *To square with genesis: casual statements and shamanic ideas in Wayãpí* (Edinburgh, 1989).

- **David Cleary**, *Anatomy of the Amazon gold rush* (Oxford, 1990).

- **Peter Silverwood-Cope**, *Os makú: povo caçador do noreste da Amazônia* (Brasília, 1990).

- **William Milliken** et al., *The ethnobotany of the Waimiri Atroari Indians of Brazil* (Kew, 1992).

- **Stephen Nugent**, *Amazonian caboclo society: an essay on invisibility and peasant economy* (Oxford, 1993).

- **Alan Tormaid Campbell**, *Getting to know Waiwai. An Amazonian ethnography* (London, 1995).

- **William Milliken** (with **Bruce Albert**), *Yanomami, a forest people* (Kew, 1999).

- **Mark Harris**, *Life on the Amazon: the anthropology of a Brazilian peasant village* (Oxford, 2000).

- **Cecilia MacCullum**, *Gender and sociality in Amazonia: how real people are made* (Oxford, 2001), on the Cashinahua people of Acre.

- **Colin McEwan**, **Cristiana Barreto** and **Eduardo Neves**, eds, *Unknown Amazon: culture in nature in Ancient Brazil* (London, British Museum, 2001).

Ecology/Environment/Development

- **Ghillean Prance** (with M.F. da Silva), *Arvores de Manaus* (Belém, 1976).

- **Nigel J.H. Smith**, *Rainforest corridors: the Transamazon colonisation scheme* (Berkeley and London, 1982).

- **Ghillean Prance** and **Thomas Lovejoy**, eds, *Amazonia* (London, 1985).

- **John Hemming**, ed., *Change in the Amazon Basin*. Vol 1 *Man's impact on forests and rivers*. Vol 2 *The frontier after a decade of colonisation* (Manchester, 1985).

- **Ghillean Prance**, ed., *Tropical forests and world climate* (London, 1986).

- **Ghillean Prance**, *Manual da botânica economica do Maranhão* (São Luís, 1988).

- **Anthony Hall**, *Developing Amazonia: deforestation and social conflict in Brazil's Carajas programme* (Manchester, 1989).
  PORTUGUESE TRANSLATION: Rio de Janeiro, Zahar, 1991.

- **David Goodman** and **Anthony Hall**, eds, *The future of Amazonia: destruction or sustainable development?* (London, 1990).

- **Michael J. Eden**, *Ecology and land management in Amazonia* (London, 1990).

- **Peter Flynn** and **H. Jaenecke**, eds, *Sustainable land use systems and human living conditions in the Amazon* (Brussels, 1992).

- **Peter A. Furley**, ed., *The forest frontier. Settlement and change in Brazilian Roraima* (London, 1994).

- **Gordon J. MacMillan**, *At the end of the rainbow? Gold, land and people in the Brazilian Amazon* (London, 1995), on settlement in Roraima in the 1980s and the early 1990s.

- **Anthony Hall**, *Sustaining Amazonia: grassroots actions for productive conservation* (Manchester, 1997).

- **Nigel J.H. Smith**, *The Amazon River Forest: a natural history of plants, animals and people* (New York and Oxford, 1999).

- **Anthony Hall**, ed., *Amazonia at the crossroads: the challenge of sustainable development* (London, Institute of Latin American Studies, 2000).

- **Nigel J.H. Smith**, *Amazon sweet sea. Land, life and water at the river's mouth* (Austin, TX, 2002).

Maracá Rainforest Project

- **John Hemming**, **James A. Ratter** and **Angelo A. dos Santos**, *Maracá* (São Paulo, 1988).

- **William Milliken** and **James A. Ratter**, eds, *The vegetation of the Ilha de Maracá* (Edinburgh, Royal Botanic Garden, 1989).

- **John Hemming** and **James A Ratter**, *Maracá — rainforest island* (London, 1993).

- **John Hemming**, ed., *The rainforest edge. Plant and soil ecology of Maracá island, Brazil* (Manchester, 1994).

- **James A. Ratter** and **William Milliken**, eds, *Maracá: the biodiversity and environment of an Amazonian rainforest* (London, 1998).

BIBLIOGRAPHY

- **Leslie Bethell**, ed., *Cambridge history of Latin America*. Vol. XI *Bibliographical essays* (Cambridge, 1995) (including eighteen essays on Brazil)

- **John P. Dickenson**, *Brazil: world bibliographical series*, vol. 57 (revised edition) (Oxford and Santa Barbara, 1997).

Many of the books on Latin America in general by British scholars have much to offer on Brazil. It is impossible to list them all here. The following, however, perhaps deserve to be singled out:

- **David Joslin**, *A century of banking in Latin America* (Oxford, 1963).

- **D.C.M. Platt**, *Britain and Latin American trade, 1806–1914* (London, 1972) and *Business history, 1840–1930. An inquiry based on British experience in Latin America* (Oxford, 1977).

- **Alistair Hennessy**, *The frontier in Latin American history* (London, 1978).

- **R. A. Humphreys**, *Latin America and the Second World War, Vol. 1, 1939–42, Vol. 2, 1942–45* (London, 1981–82).

- **George Philip**, *Oil and politics in Latin America. Nationalist movements and state companies* (Cambridge, 1982).

- **Bill Albert**, *South America and the world economy from Independence to 1930* (London, 1983) and *South America and the First World War. The impact of the war on Brazil, Argentina, Peru and Chile* (Cambridge, 1988).

- **Dawn Ades**, *Art in Latin America: the modern era, 1820–1980* (London, South Bank Centre, 1989).

- **Oriana Baddeley** and **Valerie Fraser**, *Drawing the line: art and cultural identity in contemporary Latin America* (London, 1989).

- **Gerald Martin**, *Journeys through the labyrinth. Latin American fiction in the twentieth century* (London, 1989).

- **John King**, *Magical reels. A history of cinema in Latin America* (London, 1990).

- **David Lehmann**, *Democracy and development in Latin America: economics, politics and religion in the post-war period* (Oxford, 1990).

- **William Rowe** and **Vivian Schelling**, *Memory and modernity. Popular culture in Latin America* (London, 1991).

- **Edwin Williamson**, *The Penguin history of Latin America* (London, 1992).

- **Leslie Bethell** and **Ian Roxborough**, *Latin America between the Second World War and the Cold War, 1944–1948* (Cambridge, 1992).

- **Mike Gonzalez** and **David Treece**, *The gathering of voices. The twentieth century poetry of Latin America* (London, 1992).

- **Rory Miller**, *Britain and Latin America in the nineteenth and twentieth centuries* (London, 1992).

- **Victor Bulmer-Thomas**, *The economic history of Latin America since Independence* (Cambridge, 1994).

- **Rosemary Thorp**, *Progress, poverty and exclusion. An economic history of Latin America in the twentieth century* (Washington, IDB, 1998).

- **Valerie Fraser**, *Building a new world. Studies in the modern architecture of Latin America, 1930–1960* (London, 2000).

Independent scholars, journalists and travellers continued to write about Brazil — its history, culture, ecology, economy, society and politics.

- **Jack and Avril Grant White**, *Jungle down the street* (London, 1958), an account of a journey along the eastern portion of the Amazon River, with particular attention given to Belém and the island of Marajó.

- **V.S. Naipaul**, *The middle passage* (London, 1962), the first of the Trinidad-born British author's many travel books, which includes a chapter recording impressions of British Guiana and Boa Vista (Roraima) in 1960, covering much the same borderlands territory as did Evelyn Waugh in *Ninety-two days* (see p. 88).

- **Gilbert Phelps**, *The last horizon* (London, 1964). Phelps, novelist, literary critic and journalist, visited parts of Brazil often overlooked by travel writers. For example, a chapter is devoted to impressions of Ceará and another to Paraná, where the Russian-speaking author seeks out the community of Russian 'Old Believers'. Much of the book is devoted to the Amazon (especially around Belém and Manaus), and there are accounts of São Luís (Maranhão), Belo Horizonte, Blumenau (Santa Catarina), Pelotas and Santana do Livramento (Rio Grande do Sul), as well as Rio de Janeiro and São Paulo.

- **Richard Collier**, *The land that God forgot. The story of the Amazon rubber boom* (1968). The 'strange story' is reconstructed through interviews conducted during a 25,000-mile journey the author made from Rio to Manaus, the Rio Negro, Porto Velho and the Madeira–Mamore railway to Guajará-Mirim and then to Bolivia and Peru.

- **Malcolm Slesser**, *Brazil: land without limit* (London, 1969). Slesser, a chemical engineer from Glasgow, while visiting professor at the Federal University of Rio de Janeiro, lectured and travelled in many parts of Brazil (especially the state of Rio de Janeiro, São Paulo, Paraná, Minas Gerais, Brasília, Mato Grosso, Amazonia, Recife and Salvador) and recorded his impressions on Brazil's quest for modernity.

- **Peggie Benton**, *One man against the dry lands: struggle and achievement in Brazil* (London, 1972) and *The dry lands bear fruit: struggle and achievement in Brazil* (Chichester, 1993). In the 1960s Benton served at the British consulate in Rio de Janeiro. These books are accounts of the priest Lira Parente's work and community development projects in Piauí and parts of Bahia, financed by European NGOs.

- **Gordon Campbell**, *Brazil stuggles for development* (London, 1972). Campbell was *Financial Times* correspondent in Brazil 1964–70.

- **Richard Bourne,** *Getulio Vargas of Brazil, 1883–1954* (London, 1974). Bourne is also the author of *Political leaders of Latin America* (London, 1969), which includes essays on Carlos Lacerda and Juscelino Kubitschek, and *Assault on the Amazon* (London, 1978), an early account of the development of the Transamazonica Highway — with much of interest on migrants, the impact of road on colonization and Indians.

- **Benedict Allen**, *Mad white giant: a journey to the heart of the Amazon jungle* (London, 1985), an account of travels from the mouth of the Orinoco River in Venezuela to Roraima and east to Macapá (Amapá).

- **John Ure**, *Trespassers on the Amazon* (London, 1986) is a history of British and North American explorers, naturalists, investors and adventurers in the Amazon from the 16th century to the 1960s. Ure served as British ambassador to Brazil between 1984 and 1987.

- **William B. Forsyth**, *The wolf from Scotland. The story of Robert Reid Kalley — pioneer missionary* (Darlington, Co. Durham, 1988) is an admiring biography of Kalley who, along with a group of Portuguese followers fleeing religious persecution on the island of Madeira, introduced Presbyterianism to Brazil (Rio de Janeiro and Pernambuco) in the 1850s.

- **Tony Gross**, *Fight for the forest: Chico Mendes in his own words* (London, 1989). Gross served as a representative of Oxfam, the British-based NGO, in Brazil.

- **Stephen Nugent**, *Big mouth: the Amazon speaks* (London, 1990). Nugent, an academic anthropologist (see p. 112) at London's Goldsmiths' College, sets out in this very funny book to debunk many myths about Amazonia.

- **George Monbiot**, *Amazon watershed. The new environmental investigation* (London, 1991). Monbiot, journalist and environment campaigner, travelled widely in the Brazilian Amazon (especially Yanomami territory near the Venezuelan border, Tukano territory near the Colombian border and Uru Eu Wau Wau territory in Rondônia) investigating mahogany extraction and deforestation, land seizures and the murder of community activists.

- **Sue Branford** (with **Oriel Glock**), *Last frontier: fighting over land in the Amazon* (London, 1993); (with **Bernardo Kucinski**) *Brazil: carnival of the oppressed: Lula and the Brazilian Workers' Party* (London, 1995); (with **Jan Rocha**) *Cutting the wire: the story of the landless movement in Brazil* (London, 2002); and (with Bernardo Kucinski) *Politics transformed: Lula and the Workers' Party in Brazil* (London, 2003). Branford is an independent journalist who has worked for the BBC and contributed to many newspapers including the *Economist* and the *Guardian*. Jan Rocha, a São Paulo-based independent journalist and former

Guardian correspondent, is also the author of *Murder in the rainforest: the Yanomami, the gold miners and the Amazon* (London, 1999).

- **Roderick Cavaliero**, *The Independence of Brazil* (London, 1993). Cavaliero had served as director of the British Council in Rio de Janeiro.

- **N.P. Macdonald**, *The making of Brazil. Portuguese roots 1500–1822* (Lewes, Sussex, 1996). Macdonald, who was born in Brazil, had a long career as a journalist, broadcaster and information officer. He is also the author of *Land and people of Brazil* (London, 1959).

- **Brian Vale**, *Independence or death! British sailors and Brazilian Independence, 1822–25* (London, 1996) and *A war betwixt Englishman, Brazil against Argentina on the River Plate, 1825–1830* (London, 2000). Vale has also worked for the British Council in Brazil.

- **James Woodall**, *A simple Brazilian song: journeys through the Rio sound* (London, 1997) is a journalist's exploration of musical life in Rio de Janeiro. The author describes his visits to samba schools and meetings with Caetano Velloso, Chico Buarque and Gilberto Gil.

- **Aidan Hamilton**, *An entirely different game. The British influence on Brazilian football* (Edinburgh and London, 1998). Hamilton, a freelance sports writer, spent three years in Brazil researching British influence on Brazilian football from the arrival of Charles Miller in 1894 to c. 1950.

- **Peter Fryer**, *Rhythms of resistance: African musical heritage in Brazil* (London and Hannover, NH, 2000). Fryer, a veteran (Trotskyist) journalist, has produced a scholarly interpretation of African influence in Brazilian music.

- **Alex Bellos**, *Futbol: the Brazilian way of life* (London, 2001). Bellos went to Brazil in 1998 as the correspondent of the *Guardian* and *Observer* newspapers.
  PORTUGUESE TRANSLATION: Rio de Janeiro, Jorge Zahar Editor, 2003.

- **Paul Catchpole**, *A very British railway* (St Teath, Cornwall, 2002). Catchpole, an engineering enthusiast, produced a technical and photographic history of the São Paulo (Santos–Jundaí) Railway.

Finally, complementary to this survey of Brazil in books by British and Irish authors is **Oliver Marshall**, *Brazil in British and Irish archives* (Oxford, Centre for Brazilian Studies, 2002), a valuable guide to Brazil-related manuscripts and other documentary sources held by archives in Britain and Ireland.

INDEXES

Authors
Places

Authors

Abel, Clarke: 40
Ades, Dawn: 111, 115, 121
Albert, Bill: 121
Albert, Bruce: 118
Alcock, Frederick: 79
Allen, Benedict: 123
Amann, Edmund: 112, 116
Anson, George: 18
Anderson, Aeneas: 22
A.P.D.G. (anon): 38–9
Armitage, John: 51–2
Ashe, Thomas: 36
Atchison, Charles C.: 77
Atkins, John: 17
Aylmer, Fenton: 62
Baddeley, Oriana: 121
Ball, John: 75
Banner, Horace: 90
Banks, Joseph: 19–20
Barlow, Edward: 15
Barlow, Nora: 53
Barman, Roderick J.: 111, 113, 114
Barrow, John: 22
Barrington, George: 22
Bates, Henry Walter: 57–9
Bell, Alured Gray: 83
Bellos, Alex: 125
Bennett, Frank: 82–3
Benton, Peggie: 123
Bethell, Leslie: 101–2, 104–5, 113, 116, 120, 121
Bigg-Wither, Thomas Plantagenet: 73
Boddam-Whetham, J.W.: 73
Bourne, Richard: 123
Box, Ben: 84
Boxer, Charles: 96–8
Bradley, William: 21
Branford, Sue: 124
Brooks, John: 84
Brookshaw, David: 109, 114, 115
Brown, Charles Barrington: 72–3
Browne, Janet: 53
Bruce, G.J.: 83
Bryce, James: 81
Bulkeley, John: 18
Burgess, Wilson: 60
Burke, Ulrick Ralph: 75–6

Bulmer-Thomas, Victor: 115, 122
Burton, Isabel: 65–6
Burton, Jean: 67
Burton, Richard: 65–7
Bury, John: 99
Byron, John: 19
Caldcleugh, Alexander: 43
Campbell, Alan Tormaid: 111, 118
Campbell, Archibald: 39
Campbell, George: 69
Campbell, Gordon: 123
Candler, John: 60
Carlisle, Arthur Drummond: 64
Carmichael, Elizabeth: 117
Casement, Roger: 79–80
Cathchpole, Paul: 126
Cavaliero, Roderick: 125
Cavandish, Thomas: 13, 14
Chamberlain, Henry: 42–3
Christie, William Dougal: 63
Churchward, Robert: 88
Clark, Edwin: 74
Clark, Hamlet: 62
Cleary, David: 84, 111, 118
Clough, R. Stewart: 72
Conder, Josiah: 47–8
Cochrane, Thomas: 46–7
Coleridge, F.A.: 80–1
Collier, Richard: 123
Cook, James: 19–20
Cooke, Edward: 17
Coote, Walter: 75
Course, A.G.: 15
Cowell, Adrian: 100
Cummins, Geraldine: 86
Cummins, John: 18
Cunningham, Robert O.: 64
Cunningham Graham, R.B: 85
Dampier, William: 16
Darwin, Charles: 52–3
Davies, Howell: 84
De Kadt, Emanuel: 102, 105, 116
Delaney, L.T.: 82
Dent, Hastings Charles: 76
Desmond, Adrian: 53
Dickenson, John P.: 107, 116, 120
Dillon, L.: 63

Dineen, Mark: 112, 115
Domville-Fife, Charles W.: 81
Dunlop, Charles: 72
Drake, Francis: 13
Duncan, Thomas Bentley: 89
Dundas, Robert: 56–7
Dunkerley, James: 116
Eden, Michael J.: 111, 119
Ellis, Henry: 40
Elwes, Robert: 61–2
Fawcett, Brian: 86
Fawcett, Percy Harrison: 86
Feldwick, W.: 82
Findlay, Alexander George: 56
Fitzgerald, S.M.D.: 59
FitzRoy, John: 48
Flecknoe(e), Richard: 15
Fleming, Peter: 88
Flynn, Peter: 107, 116, 119
Forbes, James: 19
Forsyth, William B.: 124
Foweraker, Joe: 108, 117
Frances, May: 77
Fraser, Valerie: 121, 122
Fry, Peter: 111, 117
Fryer, Peter: 125
Furley, Peter A.: 119
Gardner, George: 55
Gibson, Christopher: 89
Gledson, John: 108, 114, 115
Gonzalez, Mike: 121
Goodman, David: 119
Gotch, Rosamund Brunel: 44
Graham, Maria: 44–6
Grant, Andrew: 35
Gribbin, John: 48
Gribbin, Mary: 48
Griffin, John: 23
Grimble, Ian: 47
Gross, Tony: 124
Grubb, Kenneth: 87
Guppy, Nicholas: 99–100
Hadfield, William: 60
Hakluyt, Richard: 14
Hall, Anthony: 107, 117, 119
Hallewell, Laurence: 114
Hambloch, Ernest: 90–1
Hamilton, Aidan: 125
Hanson, Terence C.: 87
Harris, Mark: 112, 118

Hart-Davis, Duff: 88
Harvey, Robert: 47
Hawkesworth, John: 20
Hawkins, Richard: 13, 14, 15
Hawkins, William: 13
Hemming, John: 106, 112, 113, 114, 118, 120
Henderson, James: 42
Henderson, Keith: 85
Hennessy, Alistair: 120
Henshall, Janet D.: 116
Hinchliff, Thomas Woodbine: 62
Holman, James: 50
Howarth, W.: 85
Humphrey, John: 108, 117
Humphreys, R.A.: 121
Hunter, J.A.: 84
Hunter, John: 21
Hutchinson, Thomas J.: 67
Huxley, Francis: 99
Inglis, Brian: 80
Jacaré Assu (pseud.): 71–72
Jenkins, Dilwyn: 84
Joslin, David: 120
Kennedy, A.J.: 68
Kennedy, William Robert: 78
Keith, George Mouat: 24–5
Keynes, Richard Darwin: 53
Kindersley, Mrs Nathaniel: 19
King, John: 121
Kipling, Rudyard: 86–7
Knapp, Sandra: 58
Knight, Edward Frederick: 75
Knivet, Anthony: 13, 14, 15
Koebel, W.H.: 83–4
Koster, Henry: 37–8
Lambert, Charles J.: 74
Lambert, Mrs S.: 74
Lancaster, James: 13
Lehmann, David: 112, 117, 121
Lidstone, William: 72
Lindley, Thomas: 23–4
Lisle, James George Semple: 23
Livermore, H.V. (Harold): 98–99
Lloyd, Christopher: 47
Lloyd, Reginald: 82
Lorimer, Joyce: 14, 113
Lowe, Frederick: 54
Luccock, John: 36–37
McCormack, W.J.: 80

Index: Authors

MacCullum, Cecilia: 118
Macdonald, N.P.: 125
Macdonell, Anne: 77
Macdouall, John: 48
McEwan, Colin: 118
McGuirk, Bernard: 115
Macintyre, Archibald: 85
McLeod, John: 40
McLynn, Frank: 67
MacMillan, Gordon J.: 119
Madox, Richard: 13
Mansfield, Charles Blachford: 61
Marjoribanks, Alexander: 60
Marshall, Oliver: 84, 126
Martin, Gerald: 121
Masterman, George Frederick: 67
Mathews, Edward D.: 73–4
Mathison, Gilbert Farquhar: 43
Mavor, Elizabeth: 44
Maw, Henry Lister: 49
Mawe, John: 35–6
Maxwell, Kenneth: 102, 110, 112, 113
Maybury-Lewis, David: 100
Mee, Margaret: 100
Miller, Rory: 121
Milliken, William: 118, 120
Mitchell, Angus: 80
Mitchell, Simon: 117
Momsen, R.P.: 116
Monbiot, George: 124
Moore, James: 53
Moseley, H.N.: 69
Mulhall, Edward T.: 71
Mulhall, Marian McMurrough: 71
Mulhall, Michael G.: 71
Murray, John Hale: 64
Naipaul, V.S.: 122
Nichols, Peter: 48
North, Marianne: 70–1
Nugent, Stephen: 112, 118, 124
O'Brien, Bernard: 14
Oakenfull, J.C.: 80
O'Neill, Thomas: 25
Ouseley, William Gore: 56
Parkinson, Sydney: 19–20
Paton, Alexander: 54–5
Pearce-Edgecumbe, Edward Robert: 76
Pearson, Hugh: 86
Petros (pseud.): 72
Phelps, Gilbert: 122

Philip, George: 121
Phillip, Arthur: 21
Platt, D.C.M.: 120
Ponsonby, Laura: 71
Pontiero, Giovanni: 101–2, 103–4, 114, 115
Prance, Ghillean: 111, 118, 119
Prior, James: 39
Purchas, Samuel: 14
Purdy, John: 41–2
Raby, Peter: 58
Ratter, James A.: 120
Reid, B.L: 80
Rees, Siân: 21
Rivière, Peter: 56, 102, 105–6, 114, 117
Roome, William J.W.: 89–90
Robertson, John Parish: 34–5
Robertson, William Parish: 34–5
Rocha, Jan: 124–5
Rogers, Woodes: 17
Rowe, William: 121
Roxborough, Ian: 121
Russell-Wood, A.J.R.: 102, 109–110, 112, 113
Salvin, Hugh: 47
Saumarez, Philip: 18
Sawyer, Roger: 80
Scarlett, Peter Campbell: 54
Schomburgk, Richard: 55–6
Scully, William: 63
Seaward, M.R.D.: 59
Shaw, Lisa: 112, 115
Sheffield, Roy: 88–9
Shelvocke, George: 17
Shermer, Michael: 58
Shillibeer, John: 39–40
Silverwood-Cope, Peter: 118
Sitwell, Sacheverell: 101
Slesser, Malcolm: 123
Smith, Anthony: 101
Smith, Joseph: 112, 113, 114
Smith, Nigel J.H.: 110, 118, 119
Smith, William Sidney: 34
Smyth, William: 54
Southey, Richard: 26–8
Spruce, Richard: 57–9
Spry, William James Joseph: 69
Staples Jr, Robert: 75–6
Staunton, George: 22
Stepan, Nancy Leys: 110, 113

Swainson, William: 41
Swire, Herbert: 70
Tench, Watkin: 21
Thompson, George: 67
Thomson, C. Wyville: 69
Thorp, Rosemary: 122
Tomlinson, H.M.: 81
Treece, David: 109, 114, 121
Tuckey, James: 24
Turnball, John: 23
Ure, John: 124
Vale, Brian: 125
Vaux, James Hardy: 25
Vincent, Ethel Gwendoline: 78
Wallace, Alfred Russel: 57–9
Walpole, Fred: 57
Walter, Richard: 18
Walsh, Robert: 50
Waterton, Charles: 40
Waugh, Evelyn: 88
Webster, William Henry Bayley: 49–50
Wells, James W.: 74
Wetherell, James: 61

White, Avril Grant: 122
White, Jack Grant: 122
Whitehead, Laurence: 116
Whitehead, P.J.P.: 113
Wickham, Henry Alexander: 70
Wilberforce, Edward: 60–1
Wild, John James: 69
Wileman, J.P.: 78–9
Wilkins, William Henry: 65
Williams, Claire: 112, 115
Williams, Glyn: 18
Williamson, Edwin: 121
Williamson, James A.: 87
Wilson, E.: 68
Wilson, James: 22–3
Woodall, James: 125
Woodcock, George: 59
Woodoffe, Joseph Froude: 82
Wright, Arnold: 82
Wright, Simon: 115
Wright, Walter: 77
Young, John: 19

Places

Acre: 118, 124
Alagoas: 55, 60, 65, 76, 87
Amapá: 123
Amazon: *to 1700* 14; *1808–31* 49; *1831–70* 54, 55, 57–9; *1870–1914* 70, 72, 73, 79–81, 82; *1914–45* 87, 89, 100; *1945–2003* 105–7, 110, 111, 112, 113, 114, 117, 118, 119, 120, 122, 123, 124
Angra dos Reis: 17
Araguaia (river): 88
Bahia: *1700–1807* 17, 23; *1808–31* 41, 47; *1831–70* 55, 56, 60, 62, 63; *1870–1914* 69, 74, 76, 77, 78; *1914–45* 86, 89; *1945–2003* 101, 109, 123; *see also under* 'Salvador'
Belém: *see under* 'Pará'
Belo Horizonte: 122
Blumenau: 122
Boa Vista: 81, 88, 122; *see also under* 'Roraima'
Botafogo: 54, 76, 78
Brasília: 123
Cabo Frio: 48, 53
Cafundó: 111, 117
Caruarú: 89
Ceará: 38, 55, 122
Chapada Diamantina: 86
Copacabana: 84, 87
Corumbá: 71, 86
Cuiabá: 71, 86
Curitiba: 36, 73
Descalvados: 89
Destero: *see under* 'Santa Catarina'
Diamantina: 55
Egas: 49
Espírito Santo: 47, 60, 61
Fernando de Noronha (island): 15, 38, 49, 68, 69, 70, 78
Goiás: 42, 85, 88
Gongo Soco: 50
Guanabara Bay: 15, 23
Guajará-Mirim: 82, 123
Ilha Grande: 17, 61, 78
Joazeiro: 89
Juiz da Fora: 62
Laguna: 23
Macaé: 72

Macapá: 123
Maceió: 60, 65, 76, 87; *see also under* 'Alagoas'
Madeira (river): 81, 82
Manaus: *1808–31* 49; *1870–1914* 70, 73, 74, 81, 82; *1945–2003* 111, 118, 122, 123
Maracá: 120
Maranhão: *1808–31* 42, 47, 49; *1831–70* 55; *1870–1914* 74; *1945–2003* 99, 111, 119, 122
Mangaratiba: 61
Marajó, (island): 72, 122
Martin Vas (island): 75
Mato Grosso: *1808–31* 42; *1870–1914* 71; *1914–45* 85, 86, 88, 89; *1945–2003* 100, 101, 106, 123
Minas Gerais: *1808–31* 35, 36, 37, 38, 43, 50; *1831–70* 53, 55, 60, 62, 65; *1870–1914* 70, 74, 76; *1945–2003* 101, 122, 123
Miranda: 89
Monteiro: 40
Mostardes: 23
Natal: 38, 87
Negro (river): 54, 58, 70, 123
Nova Friburgo: 43, 55, 72
Obidos: 49, 73, 82
Olinda: 39, 40, 41
Ouro Preto: 50, 55
Paquetá (island): 75, 79
Pará: *1808–1831* 34, 42, 47, 49, 50; *1831–70* 54, 57; *1870–1914* 72, 74, 81, 82; *1914–45* 88; *1945–2003* 99, 122
Paraíba: 38, 61
Paraná: 36, 48, 73, 122, 123
Paraná river: 89
Paranaguá: 48
Pelotas: 122
Pernambuco: *to 1700* 15; *1700–1808* 17; *1808–31* 37, 39, 40, 41, 42, 44–5, 47; *1831–70* 55, 60, 61, 62, 63, 64, 65, 74, 75, 78, 79, 83; *1914–45* 87; *1945–70* 101; *see also under* 'Recife'
Petrópolis: *1831–70* 60, 62, 64; *1870–1914* 71, 72, 74, 75, 76, 77; *1945–2003* 124

Piauí: 55, 123
Porto Alegre: 23, 71
Porto Seguro: 24
Porto Velho: 81, 82, 123
Recife: 13, 39, 40, 76, 85, 123; *see also under* 'Pernambuco'
Riberão Prêto: 88
Rio Grande do Sul: 23, 37, 42, 71, 72, 77, 83, 122
Rio de Janeiro: *to 1700* 15; *1700–1807* 18, 19, 20, 21, 22, 24, 25; *1808–1831* 34, 35, 36, 37, 38, 39, 40, 42, 43, 44–6, 47, 48, 49, 50; *1831–70* 52–3, 54, 55, 56, 57, 60, 61, 62, 63, 64, 66; *1870–1914* 70, 71, 74, 75, 76, 77, 78, 79, 83; *1914–45* 84, 85, 87, 88, 90; *1945–2003* 101, 122, 123, 124, 125; *see also under* 'Botafogo', 'Copacabana' and 'Guanabara Bay'
Rondônia: 81, 82, 123, 124
Roraima: 55–6, 73, 81, 88, 100, 105–6, 114, 117, 122, 123
Salto de Pirapora: *see under* 'Cafundó'
Salvador: *to 1700* 16; *1700–1807* 17, 19, 23, 24, 25; *1808–31* 39, 42; *1831–70* 56–7, 60, 61, 62, 64; *1870–1914* 69, 76, 77, 78, 79; *1914–45* 85, 89; *1945–2003* 123; *see also under* 'Bahia'

Santa Catarina: 13, 17, 18, 35, 37, 42, 48, 49
Santa Cruz (Rio de Janeiro): 43
Santana do Livramento: 122
Santarém: 49, 54, 57, 73, 82
Santos: 13, 48, 61, 65–6, 78, 79, 87
São Francisco do Sul: 36
São Francisco (river): 41, 65
São Francisco (valley): 89
São Leopoldo: 72
São Luís: *see under* 'Maranhão'
São Paulo: *1808–31* 48; *1831–70* 65; *1870–1914* 75, 76, 78, 79, 83; *1914–45* 87, 88; *1945–2003* 111, 117, 122, 123, 126
São Vicente: 13,
Tabitinga: 49, 54, 72
Tapirape (river): 88
Teresópolis: 62
Tocantins (river): 88
Torres: 23
Trinidade (island): 75, 78
Uruguaiana: 77
Vitória: 60; *see also under* 'Espírito Santo'
Xingu (river and region): 89, 90, 100

www.ingramcontent.com/pod-product-compliance
Lightning Source LLC
Chambersburg PA
CBHW022014160426
43197CB00007B/422